# ELECTRIC MOTORCYCLES 2019

BY
MICAH TOLL

Printed in the United States of America
Toll Publications, 2019
ISBN 978-0-9899067-2-2

*To my wife Sapir, whose patience with me is admirable in its vastness…*

# Table of Contents

A quick note to the reader:

For the electric motorcycles, dirt bikes and scooters featured in this book, every effort has been made to provide the most current performance and technical specification data. When possible, the specifications are taken directly from the manufacturers. Occasionally, this could result in figures that differ somewhat from actual performance. For example, manufacturers are sometimes guilty of overstating range and understating charging time.

In these cases where performance data has not been provided by the manufacturer and the manufacturer has not agreed to provide such data, as is sometimes the case with acceleration data, an attempt has been made to ascertain this information from vehicles available to the public.

All measurements are presented in both English and metric. For ease of comparison, metric units are presented first, even for vehicles from US-based companies whose parameters have been provided in English units. Parameters that have been converted to the alternate standard have been rounded accordingly.

Additionally, all prices have been converted to USD ($) for ease of comparison among vehicles from different countries, and conversion rates are accurate as of early 2019. For vehicles available in multiple markets, a range of prices is provided.

The vehicles in this book are presented in no particular order. No manufacturers paid any money to be included. All vehicles in this book were hand-picked based on their merits.

# Electric Motorcycles

Electric motorcycles are perhaps one of the most exciting niches within the entire electric vehicle industry. The powerful acceleration and design freedom that the shift to an electric drivetrain provide have opened up entirely new possibilities in the motorcycling world.

As cities become more crowded, an increasing proportion of commuters are looking to two-wheeled transportation. Electric motorcycles have become a natural solution to this problem. In addition to providing a more effective and efficient form of transportation as compared to cars, they are also much more enjoyable to ride. The simplicity and low maintenance of electric motorcycles also mean riders spend more time riding and less time and money wrenching or taking their vehicles in for repair.

But commuting is not the only use for electric motorcycles. From cruisers to sport bikes to racing bikes, electric motorcycles have found success in a variety of categories. Included in this section of the book are electric motorcycles that fit into all of these groups and more.

In these pages are a selection of electric motorcycles that are currently available around the world. This book covers *nearly* all available electric motorcycles, however this is not an exhaustive list. Further, an attempt has been made to include models from a wide variety of countries and manufacturers.

In addition to the electric motorcycles presented here, there are a number of other models in various stages of development that are not yet available to the public. For electric motorcycles that are nearing production or have been announced but not yet fully developed, see the Coming Soon section near the end of the book.

Zero FXS ZF7.2

# Zero S

California-based Zero Motorcycles has been building electric motorcycles since 2006. The company introduced the first production-scale electric motorcycles in the US and essentially created the modern day electric motorcycle industry.

The Zero S is the company's entry-level sport bike and is available with two different battery capacities: 7.2 kWh or 14.4 kWh. The larger battery size also offers higher motor power and slightly higher torque at the expense of reduced cargo space.

Zero also offers the Power Tank add-on to the ZF14.4 model which adds an extra 3.6 kWh and increases its range, as well as the Charge Tank add-on which adds Level 2 charging ability at up to 6 kW.

The Zero S is an excellent and affordable introductory electric motorcycle for anyone who requires a full size commuter-level electric motorcycle capable of highway speeds.

While not the most powerful electric motorcycle out there, the Zero S line is still plenty sporty for everyday thrill riding. But for those seeking a more powerful street experience, the Zero SR is likely a better choice.

**Zero S ZF7.2**
**Motor power:** 34 kW (46 hp)
**Torque:** 106 Nm (78 lb-ft)
**Top speed:** 158 km/h (98 mph)
**Range:** City - 143 km (89 mi)
           Highway - 71 km (45 mi)
**Acceleration:** Not published
**Battery capacity:** 7.2 kWh
**Removable battery?:** No
**Charge time:** 5.2 hours on Level 1
           accessory chargers drop
           time to 1.5 hours
**Weight:** 142 kg (313 lb)
**Price:** $10,995

**Zero S ZF14.4**
**Motor power:** 45 kW (60 hp)
**Torque:** 110 Nm (81 lb-ft)
**Top speed:** 158 km/h (98 mph)
**Range:** City - 288 km (179 mi)
           Highway - 145 km (90 mi)
**Acceleration:** Not published
**Battery capacity:** 14.4 kWh (18.0 kWh with optional
           Power Tank)
**Removable battery?:** No
**Charge time:** 9.8 hours on Level 1, Charge Tank or
           accessory chargers drop time to 2.5 hours
**Weight:** 185 kg (408 lb)
**Price:** $13,995

# Zero SR

The Zero SR is a higher power version of the Zero S. Like the Zero S, it also takes the form of a naked street bike.

The increased torque and power of the Zero SR create much higher performance and a more thrilling ride. The Zero SR is appropriate for those seeking quicker bottom-end acceleration. The Zero SR is also able to tackle larger hills more quickly due to its higher power controller.

Both the Zero S and SR make use of Zero's smartphone app connectivity that allows riders to monitor their bikes and make adjustments to performance such as regenerative braking strength and maximum speed or torque limits.

Instant adjustment of such performance parameters can help newer riders acclimate to the bike before experiencing the full potential of the high performance motors.

**Zero SR ZF14.4**
**Motor power:** 52 kW (70 hp)
**Torque:** 157 Nm (116 lb-ft)
**Top speed:** 164 km/h (102 mph)
**Range:** City - 288 km (179 mi)
Highway - 145 km (90 mi)
**Acceleration:** 0-97 km/h (0-60 mph) in 3.3 seconds
**Battery capacity:** 14.4 kWh (18.0 kWh with optional Power Tank)
**Removable battery?:** No
**Charge time:** 9.8 hours on Level 1, or 2.5 hours with Charge Tank or accessory chargers
**Weight:** 188 kg (414 lb)
**Price:** $16,495

# Zero SR/F

The Zero SR/F is the newest electric motorcycle in Zero's lineup and was unveiled in February of 2019. With a 82 kW motor and 200 km/h (124 mph) top speed, it is also the most powerful and fastest bike offered by Zero.

**Zero SR/F**
**Motor power:** 82 kW (110 hp)
**Torque:** 190 Nm (140 lb-ft)
**Top speed:** 200 km/h (124 mph)
**Range:** City - 260 km (161 mi)
        Highway - 159 km (99 mi)
**Acceleration:** Not published
**Battery capacity:** 14.4 kWh (18.0 kWh with optional
        Power Tank)
**Removable battery?:** No
**Charge time:** 8 hours on Level 1, or 1 hour with
        Charge Tank and dual 3 kW chargers
**Weight:** 220 kg (485 lb)
**Price:** $18,995-$20,995

The new Zero SR/F also offers the fastest charging capability of any Zero motorcycle. While the base mode offers a single 3 kW charger, that can recharge the bike in 4 hours on 220 V, the premium mode includes a second 3 kW charger to cut the charge time in half. An optional Charge Tank can be added for another 6 kW of charging power, resulting in a 0 to 95% charge time of just 1 hour with a Level 2 charger.

The Zero SR/F also employs a number of new high tech features including Zero's new Cypher III operating system and Bosch's Motorcycle Stability Control. The SR/F is also the first production electric motorcycle available that is fully Internet-of-Things connected. Users have full control of adjustable performance parameters via Zero's new smartphone app and the company can remotely provide over-the-air updates directly to the bike.

The heart of the SR/F is its new ZForce 75-10 motor, the largest motor Zero has produced to date. It is coaxially mounted, sharing the same axis as the rear swingarm and thereby resulting in constant belt tension and enhanced performance.

The Zero SR/F will begin to ship in April 2019.

# Zero DS

# Zero DSR

The Zero DS and DSR models feature the same electrical internals as their street-only Zero S and SR counterparts, including the same motor and battery options. However, the DS and DSR models are dual-sport bikes optimized for both on- and off-road riding. Not quite a standard adventure bike, they still hold their own on varied terrains.

The ability to quickly change performance parameters via Zero's smartphone app means that the bikes can be rapidly reconfigured for optimal performance on nearly any terrain. However, like all of Zero's bikes, the air-cooled motor can sometimes overheat under strenuous riding conditions. This scenario forces the bike into the lower power 'limp mode' until the motor cools to a safe level. While most riders won't see this condition under ordinary usage, it can occur during more rigorous off-road sessions.

### Zero DS ZF7.2
**Motor power:** 34 kW (46 hp)
**Torque:** 106 Nm (78 lb-ft)
**Top speed:** 158 km/h (98 mph)
**Range:** City - 132 km (82 mi)
Highway - 63 km (39 mi)
**Acceleration:** Not published
**Battery capacity:** 7.2 kWh
**Removable battery?:** No
**Charge time:** 5.2 hours on Level 1
accessory chargers drop
time to 1.5 hours
**Weight:** 144 kg (317 lb)

### Zero DS ZF14.4
**Motor power:** 45 kW (60 hp)
**Torque:** 110 Nm (81 lb-ft)
**Top speed:** 158 km/h (98 mph)
**Range:** City - 262 km (163 mi)
Highway - 126 km (78 mi)
**Acceleration:** Not published
**Battery capacity:** 14.4 kWh (18.0 kWh with optional
Power Tank)
**Removable battery?:** No
**Charge time:** 9.8 hours on Level 1, Charge Tank or
accessory chargers drop time to 2.5 hours
**Weight:** 187 kg (413 lb)
**Price:** $13,995

### Zero DSR ZF14.4
**Motor power:** 52 kW (70 hp)
**Torque:** 157 Nm (116 lb-ft)
**Top speed:** 164 km/h (102 mph)
**Range:** City - 262 km (163 mi)
Highway - 126 km (78 mi)
**Acceleration:** Not published
**Battery capacity:** 14.4 kWh (18.0 kWh with optional
Power Tank)
**Removable battery?:** No
**Charge time:** 9.8 hours on Level 1, Charge Tank or
accessory chargers drop time to 2.5 hours
**Weight:** 190 kg (419 lb)
**Price:** $16,495

# Zero FX                    Zero FXS

The Zero FX is the most affordable of Zero's lineup. That affordability comes mostly at the expense of motor power and range. With a smaller motor and battery pack than Zero's other bikes, the FX is best suited for those riders who don't require the highest speeds or power.

The FX is still a great performing bike, and in Sport mode it can still pop a wheelie or tear away from the line. The smaller and lighter bike is also the most agile of Zero's offerings and better for riders who are looking for the most responsive and maneuverable bike in Zero's lineup.

The FX also offers the option of a modular battery system. The FX ZF3.6 Modular variant comes with a single removable 3.6 kWh battery pack and space for a second pack. That provides for two options: riders can keep spare batteries charging in order to swap them on the fly and get more track time, or riders can remove the batteries to charge them remotely. Remote charging makes this version of the bike perfect for anyone who needs to charge in their apartment or office when an outlet in a parking lot may be difficult to find.

When a rider does find an outlet though, the only thing he or she will need to charge the bike is an extension cord. The FX includes a built-in 650 W charger that turns every 110 V outlet into a charging station.

While the modular option has its advantages, the ZF7.2 is more economical as compared to the ZF3.6 with an additional battery module.

The FX is equally suited for on- or off-road riding. For riders that don't desire to leave the asphalt, the Zero FXS is the street-only version. The FXS is optimized for city and highway use, and thus gets between 5-10% greater range than the FX. Both options include essentially the same motors, batteries and electronics.

---

**Zero FX ZF3.6**
**Motor power:** 20 kW (27 hp)
**Torque:** 106 Nm (78 lb-ft)
**Top speed:** 137 km/h (85 mph)
**Range:** City - 74 km (46 mi)
      Highway - 31 km (19 mi) with single battery
**Acceleration:** Not published
**Battery capacity:** 3.6 kWh (or 7.2 kWh with 2 batteries)
**Removable battery?:** Yes
**Charge time:** 5.1 hours on Level 1, accessory chargers drop time to 1.6 hours
**Weight:** 112 kg (247 lb)
**Price:** $8,495 ($11,390 with additional 3.6 kWh module)

---

**Zero FX ZF7.2**
**Motor power:** 34 kW (46 hp)
**Torque:** 106 Nm (78 lb-ft)
**Top speed:** 137 km/h (85 mph)
**Range:** City - 146 km (91 mi)
      Highway - 63 km (39 mi)
**Acceleration:** Not published
**Battery capacity:** 7.2 kWh
**Removable battery?:** No
**Charge time:** 9.7 hours on Level 1, accessory chargers drop time to 1.8 hours
**Weight:** 131 kg (289 lb)
**Price:** $10,495

---

**Zero FXS ZF3.6**
**Motor power:** 20 kW (27 hp)
**Torque:** 106 Nm (78 lb-ft)
**Top speed:** 137 km/h (85 mph)
**Range:** City - 80 km (50 mi)
      Highway - 32 km (20 mi) with single battery
**Acceleration:** Not published
**Battery capacity:** 3.6 kWh (or 7.2 kWh with 2 batteries)
**Removable battery?:** Yes
**Charge time:** 5.1 hours on Level 1, accessory chargers drop time to 1.6 hours
**Weight:** 114 kg (251 lb)
**Price:** $8,495 ($11,390 with additional 3.6 kWh module)

---

**Zero FXS ZF7.2**
**Motor power:** 34 kW (46 hp)
**Torque:** 106 Nm (78 lb-ft)
**Top speed:** 137 km/h (85 mph)
**Range:** City - 161 km (100 mi)
      Highway - 64 km (40 mi)
**Acceleration:** Not published
**Battery capacity:** 7.2 kWh
**Removable battery?:** No
**Charge time:** 9.7 hours on Level 1, accessory chargers drop time to 1.8 hours
**Weight:** 133 kg (293 lb)
**Price:** $10,495

# Harley-Davidson LiveWire

Harley-Davidson first announced its LiveWire electric motorcycle in 2014, when it showed off an early prototype to the media. Harley-Davidson even began offering test rides on the original prototype, showing support for its first and only electric motorcycle concept, but progress appeared to stall shortly afterwards.

---

**Harley-Davidson LiveWire**
**Motor power:** Not available at time of publishing
**Torque:** Not available at time of publishing
**Top speed:** 177 km/h (110 mph)
**City range:** 225 km (140 mi)
**Acceleration:** 0-60 mph in 3.5 seconds
**Battery capacity:** Not available at time of publishing
**Removable battery?:** No
**Charge time:** 80% in 40 minutes with DC fast charging
**Weight:** Not available at time of publishing
**Price:** $29,799

---

It wasn't until November of 2018 that Harley-Davidson finally unveiled its production prototype of the LiveWire and announced that pre-orders would begin in early 2019, with deliveries in Fall of 2019. While specs related to the motor and battery were not available at the time of publishing, they are expected to be announced in mid-2019.

The Harley-Davidson LiveWire offers performance that is mid-range for the industry, including a top speed of 177 km/h (110 mph) and city range of 177 km (110 mi). But despite the mid-level performance, the LiveWire includes impressive high end components and built-in technology. The LiveWire is the first electric motorcycle with an on-board LTE connection. Harley-Davidson partnered with Panasonic to build a smartphone app that syncs with the LiveWire to report vehicle data and allow users to update settings on the bike. The 4.3 inch TFT touchscreen display also offers turn-by-turn GPS navigation in addition to displaying standard info such as battery charge level and speed. The display can be further customized by the rider to show info such as music selection, alerts, notifications, etc.

The LiveWire also features high tech safety advancements including Bosch's cornering anti-lock brake system and dynamic traction control. The longitudinally-mounted motor design on the LiveWire is unconventional for an electric motorcycle and further distinguishes the LiveWire from the competition.

The LiveWire initially received heat for being introduced with a high price tag of $29,799, considering the bike's otherwise commuter-level performance. But Harley-Davidson positions the LiveWire as their premium model and plans to introduce four additional light electric motorcycles, scooters and bikes by 2022. Those vehicles are intended to broaden Harley-Davidson's market reach with more affordable vehicles.

# Evoke Urban Series

Evoke Motorcycles is a Beijing-based manufacturer founded by Western expats who sought to develop a range of affordable electric motorcycles. The company's production partner is Foxconn, the massive manufacturer of high quality electronics such as Apple iPhones. Evoke claims that their motorcycles are manufactured to match US DOT and European EEC regulations, though the bikes are not yet certified for approval and homologation in those markets.

Evoke originally began with lower speed electric motorcycles designed purely for city commuting, but introduced their Urban S model in 2016 and followed up with the similarly spec'd Urban Classic model in 2017. With a top speed of 130 km/h (81 mph), the Urban series is highway capable.

The Urban series of bikes is loosely comparable to Zero's line of electric motorcycles, albeit with somewhat lower speeds. They both target similar markets despite Evoke's models having reduced performance compared to Zero.

For now, Evoke's electric motorcycles are only available in China. However, the company is working hard to expand availability into Europe and North America.

> **Evoke Urban Series**
> **Motor power:** 19 kW (25.5 hp) peak
> 11 kW (14.8 hp) continuous
> **Torque:** 116.6 Nm (86 lb-ft)
> **Top speed:** 130 km/h (81 mph)
> **Range:** 200 km (124 mi) at 35 km/h (22 mph)
> 120 km (75 mi) at 80 km/h (50 mph)
> **Acceleration:** 0-97 km/h (0-60 mph) in 6 seconds
> **Battery capacity:** 7.8 kWh
> **Removable battery?:** No
> **Charge time:** 4 hours on 220 VAC
> 8 hours on 110 VAC
> DC fast charging available
> **Weight:** 169 kg (372.5 lbs)
> **Price:** ~$9,500

Evoke is also currently working on a cruiser style electric motorcycle known as the Evoke 6061, which was originally intended to be unveiled in late 2018. However, delays have pushed that timeframe back. The Evoke 6061 is expected to feature a high power 120 kW motor and reach greater speeds than the Urban Series bikes. However, it likely won't be ready for deliveries before 2020. For now, Evoke's Urban electric motorcycles have proven sufficiently popular to keep the company going while they bring their cruiser design to market.

# Lightning LS-218

Lightning Motorcycles, based in San Jose, California, was founded in 2006 and began operations when it converted a Yamaha R1 into a 44.7 kW (60 hp) electric racing motorcycle capable of a top speed of 161 km/h (100 mph).

**Lightning LS-218**
**Motor power:** 150 kW (201 hp)
**Torque:** 228 Nm (168 lb-ft)
**Top speed:** 351 km/h (218 mph) with highest speed gearing option and fairing
**Range (highway):** 161 km (100 mi)
**Range (mixed city/highway):** Max of 290 km (180 mi) with 20 kWh battery option
**Acceleration:** 0-97 km/h (0-60 mph) in 2.2 seconds
0-161 km/h (0-100 mph) in 5.5 seconds
**Battery capacity:** 12 kWh, 15 kWh and 20 kWh options
**Removable battery?:** No
**Charge time:** 30 min on DC fast charger
2 hours on Level 2 charger
**Weight:** 224.5 kg (495 lb)
**Price:** $38,888-$46,888 depending on battery option

Lightning continued with the development of their own in-house electric superbike, the LS-218. In 2012 it set a new record for fastest electric motorcycle with a top speed of 351 km/h (218 mph). That makes the LS-218 not just the fastest electric motorcycle, but also one of the fastest production motorcycles, period.

The LS-218 is available for purchase with different gearing options. The fastest option enables the superbike to achieve its maximum speed under the proper conditions and when outfitted with an ultra-high speed fairing.

Lightning Motorcycles used their development experience gained from the LS-218 to create a second electric motorcycle model intended as a more affordable electric sport bike. In January 2019, the company announced the Lightning Strike, which would offer 241 km (150 mi) of range and a 241 km/h (150 mph) top speed, with a price starting of just $12,998.

# Lightning Strike

The Lightning Strike builds upon Lightning Motorcycle's decade of experience with electric racing motorcycles. When announced in early 2019, the Strike was pitched as one of the most affordable high speed electric sport bikes available anywhere in the world. It sent shockwaves through the industry, which had grown accustomed to higher priced electric motorcycles.

When finally unveiled in late March of 2019, the Lightning Strike marked a significant shift in the industry. The Strike provides greater range and speed than many Zero electric motorcycles (Lightning's main competitor) at a lower price point.

**Lightning Strike Standard**
**Motor power:** 67 kW (90 hp)
**Torque:** 245 Nm (180 lb-ft)
**Top speed:** 217 km/h (135 mph)
**Range:** City - 161 km (100 mi)
        Highway - 113 km (70 mi)
**Acceleration:** Not yet published
**Battery capacity:** 10 kWh
**Removable battery?:** No
**Charge time:** 2 hours on Level 2
**Weight:** 206 kg (455 lb)
**Price:** $12,998

**Lightning Strike Carbon Edition**
**Motor power:** 90 kW (120 hp)
**Torque:** 245 Nm (180 lb-ft)
**Top speed:** 241 km/h (150 mph)
**Range:** City - 322 km (200 mi)
        Highway - 241 km (150 mi)
**Acceleration:** Not yet published
**Battery capacity:** 20 kWh
**Removable battery?:** No
**Charge time:** 35 min on DC fast charge
        3.5 hours on Level 2
**Weight:** 220 kg (485 lb)
**Price:** $19,998

Lightning offers a base model of the Strike with a slightly lower top speed of 217 km/h (135 mph) and a range of up to 161 km (100 mi). A mid-range option increases the battery capacity by 50%, while the premium Carbon Edition bumps the speed to 241 km/h (150 mph) and offers double the range of the base model. The premium Carbon Edition includes Level 3 DC fast charging as standard, while the other two models offer it as an option.

The motor and controller are liquid cooled and were developed using experience gained from the company's LS-218 electric superbike. Final assembly of the Strike primarily takes place at Lightning's California factory while production of most components occurs in the company's second factory in China.

The Strike Carbon Edition will be the first version available to customers and will begin shipping later this year.

# Energica Ego

Energica Motor Company, founded in 2010, is the first Italian manufacturer of electric supersport motorcycles and currently offers 3 models.

**Energica Ego**
**Motor power:** 107 kW (143.5 hp)
**Torque:** 200 Nm (148 lb-ft)
**Top speed:** 241 km/h (150 mph)
**Range:** 150 km (93 mi) mixed city/highway
up to 200 km (125 mi) in ECO mode
**Acceleration:** 0-97 km/h (0-60 mph) in 3 seconds
**Battery capacity:** 11.7 kWh lithium polymer
**Removable battery?:** No
**Charge time:** 0-85% in 25 min with DC fast charge
0-100% in 3.5 hours on Level 2 or 3
**Weight:** 258 kg (567 lb)
**Price:** $22,565

The Energica Ego is the company's sportiest offering, and includes a 107 kW oil cooled motor and single speed transmission. Without the need to shift, it accelerates faster than most gas-powered sport bikes to an electronically limited top speed of 241 km/h (150 mph).

An advanced feature found in the Energica Ego (and all other Energica models) is the sophisticated Vehicle Control Unit (VCU) developed in-house. The VCU monitors all electrical components including the throttle, battery, inverter, charger and the Bosch anti-lock brakes. The VCU monitors and adjusts motor power by reading throttle input 100 times per second at a resolution down to 1/100th of a degree.

The Ego can connect with a smartphone over Bluetooth. UMTS long range connection technology is currently under development. The bike also includes an on-board 3 kW Level 1 charger to allow charging from a standard electrical outlet, but can also be charged much more quickly using Level 2 or 3 charging. Brembo brakes, a Marzocchi suspension fork and Bitubo rear mono shock are standard, but Energica offers an Öhlins front and rear suspension upgrade for $3,300.

# Energica Eva 107

**Energica Eva 107**
**Motor power:** 107 kW (143.5 hp)
**Torque:** 200 Nm (148 lb-ft)
**Top speed:** 201 km/h (125 mph)
**Range:** 150 km (93 mi) mixed city/highway
      up to 200 km (125 mi) in ECO mode
**Acceleration:** 0-97 km/h (0-60 mph) in 3 seconds
**Battery capacity:** 11.7 kWh lithium polymer
**Removable battery?:** No
**Charge time:** 0-85% in 25 min with DC fast charge
      0-100% in 3.5 hours on Level 2 or 3
**Weight:** Not published
**Price:** $21,656

Electronically and structurally, the Energica Eva 107 is nearly identical to the Energica Ego. The main difference is that the Eva 107 has reduced, electronically-limited top speed of just 201 km/h (125 mph). Otherwise, the two bikes sport the same battery, motor and electronics.

However, the Eva 107 is more of a streetfighter variant. It has reduced fairings, higher handlebars and a slightly higher seat. Those differences make the Eva 107 easier to handle. Visually, those differences also make the Eva 107 appear more at home on the streets than at the track.

Similar to the Ego, the Eva 107 offers all of the same high tech features, sporty performance and high end upgrade options, but with a reduced top speed. Thus, the Eva 107 is likely a better option for everyday riders as opposed to amateur/professional racers.

# Energica Eva EsseEsse9

The Energica Eva EsseEsse9 takes an old school naked bike design approach. It lacks a front fairing, instead relying on the large round headlight to lead its design cues. It also has the highest bars of the three models, providing for a more upright riding posture reminiscent of scrambler bikes.

The EsseEsse9 has a lower power 80 kW (107 hp) motor compared to the previous two Energica models, though the top speed remains electronically limited to 201 km/h (125 mph). In most other ways, the EsseEsse9 is identical to the other Energica models. It features the same frame, batteries, electronics, color screen, brakes and suspension. The EsseEsse9 also offers Pirelli Phantom tires instead of the higher performance Pirelli Diablo Rosso IIIs found on the Ego and Eva 107.

The EsseEsse9 bike is best suited for riders seeking the high performance and high tech design offered by Energica, but in a package that offers the more comfortable feel of a scrambler or roadster.

**Energica Eva EsseEsse9**
**Motor power:** 80 kW (107 hp)
**Torque:** 180 Nm (133 lb-ft)
**Top speed:** 201 km/h (125 mph)
**Range:** 150 km (93 mi) mixed city/highway
      up to 200 km (125 mi) in ECO mode
**Acceleration:** Not published
**Battery capacity:** 11.7 kWh lithium polymer
**Removable battery?:** No
**Charge time:** 0-85% in 25 min with DC fast charge
      0-100% in 3.5 hours on Level 2 or 3
**Weight:** Not published
**Price:** $20,930

# Super SOCO TS

**Super SOCO TS**
**Motor power:** 1.95 kW-2.4 kW (2.6-3.2 hp)
**Torque:** 120 Nm (88.5 lb-ft)
**Top speed:** 65 km/h (40 mph)
　　　　　further limited in some countries
**Range:** 80-160 km (50-100 mi) with 1 or 2 batteries in ECO mode
**Acceleration:** Not published
**Battery capacity:** 1.56 kWh (or 3.12 kWh with 2 batteries)
**Removable battery?:** Yes
**Charge time:** 7-8 hours
**Weight:** 78 kg (172 lb)
**Price:** $3,400-$4,000 (varies by market)

Super SOCO is a Chinese electric motorcycle and scooter company that specializes in urban electric two-wheelers designed especially for commuters.

The TS (also known as the TS 1200R in some markets) is a city bike with sporty styling. The TS is outfitted with different performance in various markets, with its Bosch rear hub motor rated at anywhere from 1.95-2.4 kW. The TS's unlimited top speed is 65 km/h (40 mph), but it is often limited to 45 km/h (28 mph) in Europe to comply with local moped and motorcycle licensing laws.

The bike's LCD screen is rather minimalist but provides a sleek and low-cost display option. Keep in mind that Super SOCO's bikes are designed with affordability in mind.

The TS can be outfitted with either a single or pair of 60 V 26 Ah Li-ion batteries. Despite a maximum range of 80 km (50 mi) per battery at slower speeds, actual range at speeds closer to 45 km/h (28 mph) is closer to 50 km (30 mi). Adding a second battery is a convenient way to double range, and fortunately still leaves a small amount of storage space above the battery compartment. Pillion foot pegs for passengers are available in some countries, and can be bolted on as aftermarket parts.

The Super SOCO TS is an excellent choice for urban riding. For riders who don't need higher speeds, the TS is a fun and affordable electric motorcycle that offers the feeling of sport riding while still in the city.

# Super SOCO TC

**Super SOCO TC**
**Motor power:** 3 kW (4 hp)
**Torque:** 150 Nm (110.6 lb-ft)
**Top speed:** 70 km/h (43.5 mph)
　　　　　further limited in some countries
**Range:** 80-160 km (50-100 mi) with 1 or 2 batteries in
　　　　　ECO mode
**Acceleration:** Not published
**Battery capacity:** 1.8 kWh (or 3.6 kWh with 2 batteries)
**Removable battery?:** Yes
**Charge time:** 7-8 hours
**Weight:** 84 kg (185 lb)
**Price:** $3,800-$4,600 (varies by market)

The Super SOCO TC is quite similar to the TS, but offers more of a roadster appearance than the sportier looking TS. The TC's leather seat, retro-style analog speedometer and higher handlebars all contribute to the roadster feel of the bike. An LCD screen is also included as part of the analog speedometer window, displaying range, temperature, time and riding mode.

When it comes to performance, the TC is a slight step up from the TS in power, acceleration and battery capacity. However, the range remains nearly identical.

The TC is still considered to be an urban motorcycle; however, in markets where the TS is not limited to 45 km/h (28 mph), its slightly higher speed can make the difference on some moderately faster city streets. For just a slightly higher price, many riders favor the higher speed and faster acceleration of the TC. The performance boost helps the TC feel more like a light electric motorcycle and less like an electric scooter.

# Super SOCO TC Max

The Super SOCO TC Max straddles the line between and light and medium-level electric motorcycles. With a top speed of 100 km/h (62 mph), it is highway capable, though perhaps only in the slow lane.

But don't expect to go very far at those speeds. The 100 km (68 mi) range is calculated at city speeds averaging around 48 km/h (30 mph). Traveling faster will quickly eat into the 72 V and 45 Ah Li-ion battery.
In addition to the speed and power boost, the TC Max has some impressive component upgrades. Brembo brakes are standard along with a combined braking system that links the front and rear brakes for safer braking.

Unlike the smaller TC, the TC Max uses a mid-mounted motor with belt drive, which should improve handling while reducing unsprung weight. The mid-mounted motor does reduce the frame space though, which is perhaps why the battery isn't larger than 3.24 kWh. At that size, the battery is about as large as possible while still being removable to allow for indoor charging.

**Super SOCO TC Max**
**Motor power:** 5 kW (6.7 hp)
**Torque:** 170 Nm (125 lb-ft)
**Top speed:** 100 km/h (62 mph)
**Range:** 110 km (68 mi) in ECO mode
**Acceleration:** Not published
**Battery capacity:** 3.24 kWh
**Removable battery?:** Yes
**Charge time:** 7-8 hours
**Weight:** Not published
**Price:** Projected at ~$5,100

The TC Max already has EEC approval for Europe, though DOT approval for the US is still pending at the time of printing. Production is slated to begin in Q1 of 2019, with deliveries to Europe beginning in Q2.

The TC Max's styling falls somewhere between the TC and TS models, leaving the TC Max looking the part of a sporty roadster. Its higher speed and power help the bike fill a noticeable gap in the market between scooter-level light electric motorcycles and more serious (and more expensive) 160+ km/h (100+ mph) electric motorcycles. At well under half the price of most electric motorcycles falling into the latter category, the TC Max is likely to be a great option for city commuters looking for everyday convenience as well as short highway sprints.

# Nuuk

Nuuk is a Spanish electric motorcycle company that has built three different models on a similar platform. The Urban model is optimized for city riding, the Nuuk Tracker includes features designed for sportier performance and off-road riding, and the Nuuk Cargo includes a large cargo trunk for deliveries or other commercial use.

The three motorcycle models all share the same Bosch 10.5 kW mid-mounted motor and 48 V 50 Ah batteries. The bikes come standard with two batteries to provide 4.8 kWh of total capacity. One or two extra batteries can be added to increase range to a maximum of 300 km (186 mi) in the city.

In addition to the motorcycle, Nuuk also offers a moped version of the same vehicles. The moped version has a lower top speed of 45 km/h (28 mph) and accepts a maximum of two batteries instead of four. However, it can also travel twice as far on a charge and thereby achieves the same maximum range as the motorcycle.

The Nuuk electric motorcycle and moped are both currently entering production in Spain and both should be available in late 2019.

**Nuuk 4 kW**
**Motor power:** 4 kW (5.4 hp)
**Torque:** 430 Nm (317 lb-ft)
**Top speed:** 45 km/h (28 mph)
**Range:** 150 km (93 mi) in Eco mode
 75 km (46.6 mi) in Sport mode
 can be doubled with extra battery
**Acceleration:** Not published
**Battery capacity:** 2.4 kWh (or 4.8 kWh with 2 batteries)
**Removable battery?:** Yes
**Charge time:** 4.5 hours
**Weight:** 138 kg (304 lb)
**Price:** $5,500 - $6,600 (varies by market and VAT)

**Nuuk 10.5 kW**
**Motor power:** 10.5 kW (14 hp)
**Torque:** 430 Nm (317 lb-ft)
**Top speed:** 110 km/h (68 mph)
**Range:** 150 km (93 mi) in Eco mode
 75 km (46.6 mi) in Sport mode
 can be doubled with extra batteries
**Acceleration:** 0-45 km/h (0-28 mph) in 3.7 seconds
**Battery capacity:** 2x 2.4 kWh for 4.8 kWh total; option for 2 extra batteries totaling 9.6 kWh
**Removable battery?:** Yes
**Charge time:** 4.5 hours
**Weight:** 150 kg (331 lb)
**Price:** $6,700 - $8,100 (varies by market and VAT)

# Fly Free Smart Old/Desert/Classic

Fly Free Smart is a new startup company building light electric motorcycles. Based in Long Beach, California, the company plans to debut their electric motorcycles with pre-sales via crowdfunding in mid-2019.

There are three models in the Fly Free Smart lineup: Old, Desert and Classic. All three models are built on the same frame and drivetrain with a chain-driving 3 kW mid-motor and the option for one or two removable batteries. The small frame uses a vintage design with dual shocks located on either side of the rear wheel.

Differences among the models are largely stylistic. The Old model (shown below) is based on Brat-style bikes with low bars and a cafe racer style seat. The Classic looks even more vintage and fully embraces cafe racer stylings with its retro seat and clip-on handlebars. The Desert model is outfitted with knobby off-road tires and higher handlebars with a cross beam.

**Fly Free Smart Old/Desert/Classic**
**Motor power:** 3 kW (4 hp)
**Torque:** 200 Nm (147 lb-ft)
**Top speed:** 80 km/h (50 mph) with 2 batteries
64 km/h (40 mph) with 1 battery
**Range:** 80 km (50 mi) per battery in Eco mode
**Acceleration:** Not published
**Battery capacity:** 1.8 kWh
**Removable battery?:** Yes
**Charge time:** 5-8 hours
**Weight:** Not published
**Price:** ~$7,200 (exact price not yet revealed at time of printing)

All three models are designed to function as intermediate electric motorcycles with speeds fast enough to handle standard urban and off-road riding, but not quite suitable for highways. At the time of publishing, Fly Free Smart has not yet launched their motorcycles, but they plan to begin presales later in 2019.

# CSC City Slicker

The CSC City Slicker blurs the line between electric motorcycles and scooters. The frame and riding stance are sporty like a motorcycle, yet the performance is closer to a high-powered city scooter. The City Slicker also lacks a foot brake usually found on motorcycles, and instead features two handlebar brake levers like a scooter.

**CSC City Slicker**
**Motor power:** 3.2 kW peak (4.3 hp)
**Torque:** 188 Nm (138 lb-ft)
**Top speed:** 74 km/h (46 mph)
**Range:** 60 km (37 mi) at 60 km/h (37 mph)
**Acceleration:** 0-48 km/h (0-30 mph) in 4.5 sec
**Battery capacity:** 1.8 kWh
**Removable battery?:** Yes
**Charge time:** 6-7 hours
**Weight:** 98 kg (216 lb)
**Price:** $2,495

Nonetheless, the bike rides more like a motorcycle. Riders that have experienced a larger electric motorcycle might be underwhelmed by the somewhat slower acceleration and top speed of the City Slicker. But for new riders, the City Slicker will surely bring a smile to their face.

For in-the-city trips, the City Slicker is a great bike. It is peppy enough to pull away more quickly than cars when the light turns green, but is still quite efficient. The City Slicker's battery is rather small at 1.8 kWh with enough capacity for around 56 km (35 mi) of mixed riding. But that small size also means that riders can carry the 16 kg (35 lb) battery inside or up to an apartment for convenient charging.

What the City Slicker lacks in power and range, it makes up for in price. For the cost of a decent electric bicycle, the City Slicker offers a 74 km/h (46 mph) electric motorcycle. That's impressive in its own right.

For anyone seeking a fun little bike without the cost or complexity of a full-sized motorcycle, the City Slicker is an excellent urban commuter. It provides nearly all of the utility of a scooter (perhaps without the storage space) yet in a much more fun and exciting package. Just don't expect to take it on the highway.

# Sol Motors Pocket Rocket          Sol Motors Pocket Rocket S

The Pocket Rocket electric motorcycle manufactured by Stuttgart, Germany-based Sol Motors has one of the most eye-catching designs out there. Love it or hate it, the design has won numerous awards including the German Design Award 2018, Focus Open 2018 Gold and the European Product Design Award.

The Pocket Rocket is available in two models consisting of the standard Pocket Rocket and the Pocket Rocket S. While both include the same frame and major components including suspension and brakes, the S version is capable of higher speeds due to its higher power motor. For Europeans, the lower speed version conforms to L1e requirements, while the higher speed model fits the L3e class.

The aluminum frame and minimalist design contribute to the low weight of the vehicle and result in exciting performance. Eco and Sport modes offer lower and medium levels of performance, while Wheelie mode removes the power limit and earns its name with the most powerful torque level.

The Pocket Rocket sports attractive front and rear LED lights and unique molded seat but makes few other concessions to creature comforts or accessories. Suspension is accomplished via retro-style dual shocks in the rear and a bicycle-style single crown suspension fork up front.

Sol Motors is expecting to deliver their first 100 vehicles with German homologation in the summer of 2019. The company anticipates achieving EU homologation in time to begin deliveries to the rest of Europe by the end of 2019.

---

**Sol Motors Pocket Rocket**
**Motor power:** 4 kW (5.4 hp)
**Torque:** 150 Nm (111 lb-ft)
**Top speed:** 50 km/h (31 mph)
**Range:** 50-80 km (31-50 mi) depending on riding mode
**Acceleration:** Not yet determined pending final testing
**Battery capacity:** 3+ kWh (may increase by summer '19)
**Removable battery?:** Yes
**Charge time:** Not yet finalized as of printing
**Weight:** 55 kg (121 lb)
**Price:** ~$6,000 (exact price still TBD)

---

**Sol Motors Pocket Rocket S**
**Motor power:** 6 kW (8 hp)
**Torque:** 150 Nm (111 lb-ft)
**Top speed:** 80 km/h (50 mph)
**Range:** 50-80 km (31-50 mi) depending on riding mode
**Acceleration:** Not yet determined pending final testing
**Battery capacity:** 3+ kWh (may increase by summer '19)
**Removable battery?:** Yes
**Charge time:** Not yet finalized as of printing
**Weight:** 55 kg (121 lb)
**Price:** ~$7,500 (exact price still TBD)

# Electric Dirt Bikes

CAKE Kalk OR

While electric motorcycles are beginning to encroach upon the market share of traditional gas-powered motorcycles on the street, electric dirt bikes are making similar progress on the trail.

A number of companies, ranging from small startups to large manufacturers, have recently introduced their own electric dirt bikes. The market remains rather small, likely due to the smaller size of the dirt bike industry in general as compared to the larger motorcycle industry. However, despite the small size of the electric dirt bike market, there exists a significant range in the variety of electric dirt bikes currently available.

From glorified electric mountain bikes to dedicated high-performance electric dirt bikes, the developing industry already has a number of interesting offerings. And while gas-powered dirt bikes still reign supreme in numbers on tracks and trails, electric dirt bikes are quickly making headway. Their instantaneous torque provides possibilities for hill climbing and bottom-end power that is simply not achievable in gas-powered dirt bikes of equal size. Their quiet operation also makes the riding experience more enjoyable, especially for riders who appreciate the scenery and environment surrounding their rides. And with many electric dirt bikes sporting battery packs small enough to be removable and swappable, near-continuous riding is an option not afforded to larger electric motorcycles.

# UBCO 2x2

The UBCO 2x2 is a fascinating all-terrain electric two-wheeler, though classifying it has proven difficult. Some might refer to it as more of a farm bike, dirt bike, two-wheel ATV or any number of other monikers. Labels aside, the UBCO is a formidable electric motorcycle that uses a pair of 1 kW hub motors to offer two-wheel drive. The option of front-wheel drive is helpful when off-roading, as the front tire can more effectively climb up and over obstacles.

**UBCO 2x2**
**Motor power:** 2 kW (2x 1 kW hub motors)
**Torque:** 90 Nm (66.4 lb-ft) per motor
**Top speed:** 48 km/h (30 mph)
**Range:** 120 km (75 mi)
**Acceleration:** 0-45 km/h (0-28 mph) in 8 seconds
**Battery capacity:** 2.4 kWh
**Removable battery?:** Yes
**Charge time:** 0-90% in 6 hours
**Weight:** 144 lb (65 kg)
**Price:** $5,500-$6,999 (varies by market)

New Zealand-based UBCO originally designed the 2x2 for off-road uses, but the vehicle has since been homologated for street use in the US as well as Australia and New Zealand. The 2x2 sports mirrors, a license plate holder and a full light package with blinkers, allowing it to be registered for road use. With a top speed of just 48 km/h (30 mph), it is legally considered to be a moped in many jurisdictions, even though it lacks pedals.

Despite its road-registerable status, the UBCO 2x2 is most at home on less beaten paths. The 2x2 features long travel suspension and large cargo racks in front and rear. The bike includes 17 accessory lugs distributed around the frame to allow for a wide range of aftermarket or custom gear additions.

The 50 V and 48 Ah battery is not only removable, but also offers two USB ports and a 12 V accessory outlet. Riders can charge electronic devices and power tools directly from the battery - an added benefit when riding far from civilization.

For riders who need a dependable, off-road two-wheeler that can carry cargo like an ATV but legally ride on public roads like a motorcycle, the UBCO 2x2 is not only a great option but is also one of the only options. It's not cheap, but it will get you there and back. And that counts for something!

# Alta Redshift EXR

Alta Motors was a California-based electric dirt bike manufacturer. They produced multiple models of electric dirt bikes from 2016-2018. However, after a planned investment from Harley-Davidson fell through in Fall of 2018, the company struggled to pay its bills and ultimately ceased operations a few months later. That makes the 2019 Redshift EXR the last Alta available from the 2019 model year, and likely the last Alta ever to be produced.

Announced in June of 2018, the 2019 Redshift EXR is a street-legal electric dirt bike heralded for its performance on par with gas-powered competitors. With the low-end torque inherent to electric motors, Alta performed well in many competitions with sponsored riders and the company looked to be on the path to success.

The Redshift EXR was known for its impressive hill climbing ability in competitions as well as its quick charge in just 1.5 hours with 240 VAC. The bike also offered high end components from Brembo brakes to Metzeler tires and WP suspension.

**Alta Redshift ER**
**Motor power:** 37.2 kW (50 hp)
**Torque:** 57 Nm (42 lb-ft)
**Top speed:** 114 km/h (71 mph)
**Range:** 80 km (50 mi)
**Acceleration:** Not published
**Battery capacity:** 5.8 kWh
**Removable battery?:** No
**Charge time:** 1.5 hours (240V AC)
3 hours (120V AC)
**Weight:** 124 kg (273 lb)
**Price:** $12,495

While the electric motorcycle industry will mourn Alta's passing, it is important to remember the critical role that the company played in the industry. Its electric dirt bikes were renowned for their performance and helped demonstrate that electric motorcycles weren't just environmental statements, but could actually compete with, and win against, their gas-powered brethren.

Decades from now when electric motorcycles are the norm, it should not be forgotten how they got there - by standing on the shoulders of companies like Alta Motors.

# Sur Ron MX

The Sur Ron MX, also known as the Sur Ron Light Bee or Sur Ron Firefly, is a Chinese electric motorbike designed primarily for off-road riding.

**Sur Ron MX**
**Motor power:** 6 kW (8 hp)
**Torque:** 25 Nm (18.4 lb-ft) at the motor
**Top speed:** 72 km/h (45 mph)
**Range:** 64 km (40 mi) at 48 km/h (30 mph)
**Acceleration:** Not published
**Battery capacity:** 1.9 kWh
**Removable battery?:** Yes
**Charge time:** 3.5 hours
**Weight:** 50 kg (110 lb)
**Price:** $3,900 - $5,200 (varies by market)

The Sur Ron MX uses a 6 kW mid-drive motor with two stage reduction. The primary belt reduction helps alleviate higher frequency noise while the secondary chain reduction transfers the high torque to the rear wheel.

The battery consists of Panasonic 18650 cells and is removable to allow for remote charging. The frame is made from forged aluminum and is optimized for the punishment of off-road riding. The entire bike remains unusually lightweight at just 50 kg (110 lb), making it nimble and easy to jump.

The Sur Ron MX is perhaps one of the most highly modified electric dirt bikes in existence. Not only have individual riders attempted to modify the bike, but the basic platform has been modified upon import to different countries resulting in somewhat differing specs and performance levels. Aftermarket kits are also available that can add everything from bicycle pedals to light kits with turn signals to the bikes in an effort to make them street legal.

In the world of electric dirt bikes, it is hard to find anything with more bang for your buck than the Sur Ron MX. While not the fastest or most powerful, its low price makes it a great entry-level electric bike for riders seeking cheap thrills.

# CAKE Kalk OR

The Kalk OR is Sweden-based CAKE's first production electric motorcycle, if you don't count a 50-unit limited edition run of signed Kalk bikes.

The Kalk OR is designed for trail riding and is essentially a lightweight electric dirt bike. At $13,000, it is quite expensive, but features a number of high-end components including front and rear Öhlins suspension and highway motorcycle-grade four piston hydraulic brakes. The controller also offers multiple riding modes for both lower speed/maximized range riding and unlimited power and torque settings.

The Kalk OR's frame is made from 6061 extruded aluminum that is CNC jointed before welding. The rear swingarm uses similar construction with extruded 6061 tubes. The handlebar and stem use 7000 series aluminum and incorporate an integrated dashboard with unique rotary switches for selecting riding mode and regenerative braking power.

> **CAKE Kalk OR**
> **Motor power:** 7 kW (9.4 hp) continuous
> 15 kW (20 hp) peak
> **Torque:** 42 Nm (31 lb-ft)
> **Top speed:** 75 km/h (46 mph)
> **Range:** 80 km (50 mi)
> **Acceleration:** Not published
> **Battery capacity:** 2.6 kWh
> **Removable battery?:** Yes
> **Charge time:** 2.5 hours
> **Weight:** 69 kg (152 lb)
> **Price:** $13,000

The 2.6 kWh battery is removable and can be swapped out with a spare battery to extend riding time at the track. The battery is rather small compared to some other larger electric dirt bikes, although its ability to be swapped on the fly means that its smaller size gives it a weight advantage.

The Kalk OR is an impressive collection of parts with a minimalist, industrial design. However, the unique aesthetics have been divisive and have lead to strong opinions either for and against the design.

As is true for most electric dirt bikes, the Kalk OR is not street legal. CAKE has a modified version known as the Kalk OR& that is DOT and EEC approved for the US and EU markets. The street legal Kalk OR& should be out by the end of 2019.

# Kuberg FreeRider

The FreeRider is built by the Czech company Kuberg and is their adult electric dirt bike. The company also offers a number of smaller models designed for children and young riders.

**Kuberg FreeRider**
**Motor power:** 4 kW (5.4 hp), 8 kW (10.7 hp) or 12 kW (16 hp)
**Torque:** Not published
**Top speed:** 55 km/h (34 mph) for 8 kW model
                        65 km/h (40 mph) for 12 kW model
**Range:** 30-56 km (19-35 mi) at 55 km/h (34 mph)
**Acceleration:** Not published
**Battery capacity:** 1 kWh or 1.5 kWh options
**Removable battery?:** Yes
**Charge time:** 100% in 2.5 hours
                        80% in 1 hour with fast charger option
**Weight:** 36 kg (79 lb)
**Price:** $4,900-$5,800 (varies by options and market)

Despite its tubular steel frame, the FreeRider is incredibly lightweight and nimble. The 8 kW and 12 kW motor options are massive as compared to the lightweight bike, helping the FreeRider stand near the top of the power/weight ratio totem pole for electric dirt bikes. The belt drive is rather loud, perhaps all the more noticeable without imposing engine noise to mask it. A smartphone app offers Wi-Fi control over customizable settings but requires the purchase of a separate Wi-Fi adapter.

The suspension, consisting of a 180 mm travel Manitou Dorado fork and DNM Burner rear shock, offers a surprising amount of range for the small electric dirt bike. Hydraulic Tektro Auriga brakes and 20" Maxxis Creepy Crawler tires also come standard on the bike. Altogether, the FreeRider features a good collection of components considering its relatively low price.

With options for just 1 or 1.5 kWh, the Achilles heel of the FreeRider may be its smaller battery. However, the battery is made with high power Japanese Li-ion cells, so what it lacks in size it makes up in quality. And with the small battery, weight is also kept to a minimum - a major selling point of the FreeRider.

While the FreeRider is designed for off-roading, Kuberg has also created a pavement optimized model known as the FreeRider Street. Specs for the FreeRider Street are not yet known, but should be available in late 2019.

# KTM Freeride E-XC

The KTM Freeride E-XC has not been updated since the 2018 model was revealed in late 2017. However, the electric dirt bike still packs quite a punch. Its water-cooled, slim-design ,18 kW motor feeds a two-stage reduction for high torque and powerful acceleration.

The Freeride E-XC features a composite body and a frame consisting of chromoly steel and forged aluminum. The combination of materials help the bike shed weight for maneuverability while still handling the punishment of repeated jumps.

Lifting the seat reveals the 3.9 kWh battery made from 360 Sony Li-ion cells. In Eco mode, the battery can be recharged via regenerative braking. Higher power modes disable regen, as KTM believes it could impede higher performance riding. While KTM rates the battery capacity as 1.5 hours of riding time, aggressive riding can drop that time to just over half an hour. Once the battery is depleted, it can either be charged in place or removed (via four bolts) to charge off-bike.

**KTM Freeride E-XC**
**Motor power:** 9 kW (12 hp) continuous
              18 kW (24 hp) peak
**Torque:** 42 Nm (31 lb-ft)
**Top speed:** 97 km/h (60 mph)
**Range:** "1.5 hours of riding time"
**Acceleration:** Not published
**Battery capacity:** 3.9 kWh
**Removable battery?:** Yes
**Charge time:** 1.5 hours
**Weight:** 110 kg (243 lb)
**Price:** $13,300

The Freeride E-XC's controller also benefits from the same water-cooled treatment as the motor to allow the controller to provide higher power for extended riding sessions. Two laterally-mounted radiators effectively dissipate heat while riding. The suspension on the Freeride E-XC also features quality components, including a WP 250 mm inverted fork and 260 PDS rear shock.

Unlike many other electric dirt bikes, the Freeride E-XC is street legal, at least in Europe. At this time it hasn't been homologated for on-road travel in the US.

Also, unlike most other electric dirt bikes, KTM offers a leasing program for the battery, with customers buying the bike outright but leasing the battery.

With the closing of Alta Motors last year, Austrian-based KTM is one of the few high-powered electric dirt bike manufacturers currently in operation.

# Electric Motion EM 5.7 Sport Lite     Electric Motion EM 5.7 Sport

# Electric Motion 5.7 Escape Sport

French-made Electric Motion dirt bikes are designed, engineered and manufactured entirely in-house. The company claims it has produced over 3,000 units so far and is currently working on an enlarged line of electric motorcycles. For now, they are best known for their high quality electric dirt bikes.

The entry-level Sport Lite is a smaller bike that is better suited to novice riders, while the Sport and Escape Sport models offer higher speeds and range for more advanced riders. Three different controller profiles are also available to select between low power and higher performance riding modes. The bikes employ a two-stage reduction with a primary belt drive and secondary chain drive transmission, which provides high levels of power and torque right off the line.

The 2019 EM model line features upgraded power, torque and speeds thanks to a new electric motor and controller combination. The low mounted motor and transmission provide a low center of gravity and improve handling.

**Electric Motion EM 5.7 Sport Lite**
**Motor power:** 5 kW (6.7 hp) continuous
      12 kW (16 hp) peak
**Torque:** 27 Nm (19.8 lb-ft) at motor
      500 Nm (368 lb-ft) at rear wheel
**Top speed:** 60 km/h (37 mph)
**Range:** "50 to 150 minutes"
**Acceleration:** Not published
**Battery capacity:** 1.2 kWh
**Removable battery?:** Yes
**Charge time:** 2.5 hours
**Weight:** 76 kg (168 lb)
**Price:** $11,500

**Electric Motion EM 5.7 Escape Sport**
**Motor power:** 5 kW (6.7 hp) continuous
      12 kW (16 hp) peak
**Torque:** 350 Nm (257 lb-ft) at rear wheel
**Top speed:** 75 km/h (47 mph)
**Range:** "110 to 200 minutes"
**Acceleration:** Not published
**Battery capacity:** 1.9 kWh
**Removable battery?:** Yes
**Charge time:** 3 hours
**Weight:** 79 kg (174 lb)
**Price:** $14,000

**Electric Motion EM 5.7 Sport**
**Motor power:** 5 kW (6.7 hp) continuous
      12 kW (16 hp) peak
**Torque:** 27 Nm (19.8 lb-ft) at motor
      500 Nm (368 lb-ft) at rear wheel
**Top speed:** 60 km/h (37 mph)
**Range:** "110 to 200 minutes"
**Acceleration:** Not published
**Battery capacity:** 1.9 kWh
**Removable battery?:** Yes
**Charge time:** 3 hours
**Weight:** 79 kg (174 lb)
**Price:** $13,000

# LMX 161-H

The LMX 161-H is another French-made electric MX bike. At just 42 kg (93 lb) in its road-legal format, this model falls somewhere between high-end electric mountain bikes and dedicated electric dirt bikes.

The LMX 161-H qualifies for an L1e-B designation in Europe. Riders can thus travel on public roads to reach their favorite riding parks or trails.

The LMX 161-H sports a minimalist design but packs in high quality components, including an RST Killah front suspension fork with 200 mm of travel and a DNM RCP2 rear shock. Motorcycles rims and tires are combined with high-end e-bike brakes, completing the amalgamation of off-road parts. The chain-driving mid-mounted motor provides optimal low-end power, allowing the bike to climb 45° slopes with ease. The lightweight 6061 aluminum frame is designed to take a beating without adding unnecessary weight.

> **LMX 161-H**
> **Motor power:** 3.1 kW (4.2 hp) continuous
>         6.3 kW (8.4 hp) peak
> **Torque:** Not published
> **Top speed:** 45 km/h (28 mph)
> **Range:** 80 km (50 mi) max
>      50 km (31 mi) typical
> **Acceleration:** Not published
> **Battery capacity:** 1.7 kWh
> **Removable battery?:** Yes
> **Charge time:** 3 hours
> **Weight:** 42 kg (93 lb)
> **Price:** $8,700

The LMX 161-H certainly isn't the fastest or most aggressive electric dirt bike on the market, but it very well may be the lightest. So for those who prioritize weight over all other concerns, the LMX 161-H is certainly worth a ride.

# Electric Mopeds & Scooters

Electric mopeds and scooters are perhaps one of the most utilitarian options for navigating urban centers. Their nimbleness, small size and ease of operation make them easily approachable for most commuters.

Electric scooters provide many of the benefits of electric bicycles including speed of travel, ease of parking, lack of physical effort and enjoyment of riding on two wheels. However, as true motor vehicles, electric scooters are often given more space by cars. They are also capable of higher speeds which can open up more roads and thus more riding options, further increasing their convenience.

Electric scooters are beginning to showcase a number of high tech features. Smartphone integration and wireless telemetry allow riders to check in on their scooters remotely, update settings and perform diagnostics. That same connectivity can also allow manufacturers to provide over-the-air software updates to electric scooters.

Many electric scooters can also be ridden without a motorcycle license or with just a special scooter/moped license, depending on the state or country. This can also help new riders discover the convenience and fun of electric scooters without worrying about the cost or complexity of obtaining a motorcycle license.

This section features a selection of the most popular, significant and innovative models of electric mopeds and scooters currently available around the world. While China holds a distinct edge in the industry with hundreds if not thousands of domestic electric scooter versions, it would be impossible to collect and cover them all. Therefore, a number of Chinese electric scooters are also covered here, but they are limited to the most significant and those that are available outside of China.

NIU M Series

# ONYX CTY                    ONYX RCR

ONYX, a San Francisco-based moped startup that began development of two modern day mopeds in 2017, crowdfunded them 2018 and began deliveries in early 2019.

ONYX produces the high power RCR and more moderately powered CTY mopeds in their San Francisco facility. Both have functional pedals and thus are technically electric bicycles, though with a very loose interpretation of that term. The CTY has a top speed of 48 km/h (30 mph) and is already faster than most electric bicycles. The RCR has a speed of 97 km/h (60 mph) and is effectively a light electric motorcycle.

The road legality of the two vehicles is arguable. They both feature electronic limiting to drop the speed and power to legal e-bike levels, though whether or not this meets various state laws is unclear. Either way, they are impressive machines. With a vintage moped style frame, the CTY and RCR feature dual rear coilover suspension and bench style seats. Large LED halo headlights and LED bar tail lights complete the striking aesthetic. Hydraulic front and mechanical rear disc brakes provide ample stopping power for these high speed mopeds. They also offer LCD backlit displays, wireless alarm key fobs, Bluetooth connectivity to an Android app and device charging over USB 3.0 and USB C.

Perhaps the most remarkable feature of these mopeds is the price. Both are available for much lower than nearly any other electric scooter or motorcycle with comparable performance. Of course the lack of DOT certification likely helps reduce that price.

**ONYX CTY**
**Motor power:** 2.5 kW (3.3 hp)
**Torque:** 160 Nm (118 lb-ft)
**Top speed:** 48 km/h (30 mph)
**Range:** 64 km (40 mi) at 32 km/h (20 mph)
**Acceleration:** 0-25 km/h (0-15 mph) in 5.4 seconds
**Battery capacity:** 768 Wh
**Removable battery?:** Yes
**Charge time:** 4-7 hours (varies by charger power)
**Weight:** 39 kg (85 lb)
**Price:** $2,500

**ONYX RCR**
**Motor power:** 6 kW (8 hp)
**Torque:** 182 Nm (134 lb-ft)
**Top speed:** 97 km/h (60 mph)
**Range:** 120 km (75 mi) at 32 km/h (20 mph)
**Acceleration:** 0-48 km/h (0-30 mph) in 4 seconds
**Battery capacity:** 1.66 kWh
**Removable battery?:** Yes
**Charge time:** 5-6 hours
**Weight:** 54 kg (120 lb)
**Price:** $3,250

# Gogoro S1    Gogoro S2    Gogoro 2 Deluxe/Delight/Plus

Gogoro is a Taiwanese-based electric scooter manufacturer known for its battery swapping infrastructure designed to interface with its popular electric scooters. While riders can charge batteries at home, they are encouraged to make use of a subscription battery swapping program. Over 1,000 battery swap stations are located across the country, allowing riders to pull up and swap a depleted battery for a fully charged one. Returned batteries are then charged at the station to be swapped in by future riders.

Gogoro's line of scooters includes the higher performance S Series and the more affordable 2 Series. All of the scooters, except for the S1, are built on similar steel frames with suspension forks and dual rear suspension. The S1 uses an aluminum frame, a single sided front suspension arm and rear aluminum multi-link shock. The comparatively lighter weight S1 is the fastest of Gogoro's lineup, with a top speed of 95 km/h (59 mph).

All of Gogoro's scooters feature a number of high tech features. The mid-mounted motors are liquid cooled and the hydraulic brakes use a synchronized brake system. The large color display uses a number of sensors distributed throughout the scooter to monitor performance, and diagnostics are uploaded to a connected smartphone app. The scooters are also marketed as "unstealable" as they employ fingerprint authentication and 256 bit encryption. The 2 Deluxe scooter also offers face recognition to unlock the scooter as well as a redesigned center stand that is suggested to be easier to operate.

Each of the scooters has their own unique aesthetic options including different color body panels and bolt-on accessories such as windshields and luggage racks. The 25 liter under seat storage area is large for a scooter with 2 batteries. Riders can store two open face helmets in the cargo area.

### Gogoro S1
**Motor power:** 7.2 kW (9.7 hp)
**Torque:** 27 Nm (19.8 lb-ft) at the motor
202 Nm (149 lb-ft) at the rear wheel
**Top speed:** 95 km/h (59 mph)
**Range:** 100 km (62 mi) at 40 km/h (25 mph)
125 km (78 mi) at 30 km/h (18.6 mph)
with 2 batteries
**Acceleration:** 0-50 km/h (0-31 mph) in 3.7 seconds
**Battery capacity:** 11.3 kWh (or 2.6 kWh with 2 batteries)
**Removable battery?:** Yes
**Charge time:** 2.5 - 5 hours depending on charger model, also offers battery swapping stations
**Weight:** 112 kg (247 lb) with 2 batteries
**Price:** $4,700

### Gogoro S2
**Motor power:** 7.6 kW (10.2 hp)
**Torque:** 26 Nm (19.1 lb-ft) at the motor
213 Nm (157 lb-ft) at the rear wheel
**Top speed:** 92 km/h (57 mph)
**Range:** 110 km (69 mi) at 40 km/h (25 mph)
150km (93 mi) at 30 km/h (18.6 mph)
with 2 batteries
**Acceleration:** 0-50 km/h (0-31 mph) in 3.9 seconds
**Battery capacity:** 1.3 kWh (or 2.6 kWh with 2 batteries)
**Removable battery?:** Yes
**Charge time:** 2.5 - 5 hours depending on charger model, also offers battery swapping stations
**Weight:** 122 kg (269 lb) with 2 batteries
**Price:** $3,500

### Gogoro 2 Deluxe/Delight/Plus
**Motor power:** 6.4 kW (8.6 hp)
**Torque:** 25 Nm (18.4 lb-ft) at the motor
205 Nm (151 lb-ft) at the rear wheel
**Top speed:** 90 km/h (56 mph) for Deluxe/Plus
88 km/h (54.7 mph) for Delight
**Range:** 110 km (68 mi) at 40 km/h (25 mph)
150 km (93 mi) at 30 km/h (18.6 mph)
with 2 batteries
**Acceleration:** 0-50 km/h (0-31 mph) in 4.3 seconds
**Battery capacity:** 1.3 kWh (or 2.6 kWh with 2 batteries)
**Removable battery?:** Yes
**Charge time:** 2.5 - 5 hours depending on charger model, also offers battery swapping stations
**Weight:** 122 kg (269 lb) with 2 batteries
**Price:** $2,950 - $3,200 depending on model

# KYMCO Ionex Nice 100 EV      KYMCO Ionex New Many 110 EV

Despite KYMCO being the largest scooter producer in Taiwan, the massive company waited until 2018 to finally debut electric scooters. Their Ionex line of scooters use a removable battery system similar to Gogoro's. Riders can carry multiple batteries in their scooter and charge them at public battery stations. In its current form the system is only intended for charge-while-you-wait operations, but battery swapping similar to Gogoro's should be possible using the same hardware if KYMCO decides to offer the service. In addition to the swappable batteries, KYMCO's scooters feature smaller onboard batteries that are non-removable and provide a small amount of emergency range.

The Nice 100 and New Many 110 EV offer standard scooter performance with rear hub motors. The Nice 100 EV has a simplified LCD screen while the New Many 110 EV sports a more advanced LED color display. Both scooters feature rear drum brakes instead of disk brakes, one of many concessions to affordability.

Both scooters have an innovative battery compartment that drops down into the space under the floorboard. Otherwise, KYMCO's electric scooters are rather basic as compared to some of the more technologically advanced electric scooters coming out of Asia. However, KYMCO has big plans for their Ionex brand and intendeds to introduce 10 new electric scooters over the next few years.

The company has already introduced the "Ionex Commercial" line of electric scooters built on similar frames yet designed for commercial use such as deliveries, couriers and ridesharing services. More electric scooter models designed for consumer and commercial uses are expected to follow soon.

**KYMCO Ionex Nice 100 EV**
**Motor power:** 1.5 kW (2 hp)
**Torque:** 50 Nm (36.8 lb-ft) at rear wheel
**Top speed:** 45 km/h (28 mph)
**Range:** 40 km (25 mi) per battery in Eco mode
**Acceleration:** Not published
**Battery capacity:** 625 Wh per battery
                (can carry 2 or more)
**Removable battery?:** Yes
**Charge time:** 1 hour in Ionex charge stations
**Weight:** 77 kg (170 lb)
**Price:** $1,430 after subsidies in Taiwan

**KYMCO Ionex New Many 110 EV**
**Motor power:** 3.2 kW (4.3 hp)
**Torque:** 16.5 Nm (12.1 lb-ft) at the motor
**Top speed:** 59 km/h (36.7 mph)
**Range:** 40 km (25 mi) per battery in Eco mode
**Acceleration:** Not published
**Battery capacity:** 625 Wh per battery
                (can carry 2 or more)
**Removable battery?:** Yes
**Charge time:** 1 hour in Ionex charge stations
**Weight:** 94 kg (207 lb)
**Price:** $1,600 after subsidies in Taiwan

# Super SOCO CUx

Shanghai-based Super SOCO is perhaps best known for their TS, TC and TC Max electric motorcycles, but the CUx scooter is admirable in its own right. A Bosch motor, unique pyramid shaped battery and combined hydraulic brakes elevate the CUx to a status above the standard run-of-the-mill Chinese-manufactured electric scooters.

The CUx also features a front camera with full HD and night vision that can be used either for recording fun riding videos or for security. The scooter's built-in G sensor can detect a crash and will automatically save the ride video and send it to a mobile phone.

The scooter includes storage under the seat, though much of this is taken up by the uniquely shaped battery. The dashboard is a high resolution digital display. The scooter can be activated using a wireless remote key. The headlights include two C-shaped light bars that spread out across the front fairing over the handlebars. The tail lights include long LED wings that flow down the back of the scooter, providing excellent visibility from the rear and adding to the stylish design of the scooter. A grab bar is also placed just behind the seat to give passengers a more confident hold.

**Super SOCO CUx**
**Motor power:** 1.3 kW (1.75 hp) continuous
2.8 kW (3.75 hp) peak
**Torque:** 115 Nm (85 lb-ft)
**Top speed:** 45 km/h (28 mph)
**Range:** 75 km (46.6 mi)
**Acceleration:** Not published
**Battery capacity:** 1.8 kWh
**Removable battery?:** Yes
**Charge time:** 7 hours
**Weight:** 70 kg (154 lb)
**Price:** ~$3,400 (varies by market)

# NIU NGT

NIU is the largest Chinese electric scooter company and has been building scooters for years. NIU has received great acclaim both inside and outside of Asia. The company has consistently led the electric scooter industry in affordable yet technology-packed and high performance scooters. NIU scooters are known for their high quality Bosch motors and Panasonic batteries. However, the models developed for domestic sales feature domestic components including a locally developed motor.

> **NIU NGT**
> **Motor power:** 3 kW (4 hp)
> **Torque:** 180 Nm (132 lb-ft)
> **Top speed:** 70 km/h (43.5 mph)
> **Range:** 170 km (106 mi) in ECO mode with 2 batteries
> **Acceleration:** 0-40 km/h (0-25 mph) in 4.5 seconds
> **Battery capacity:** 2.1 kWh (4.2 kWh with 2 batteries)
> **Removable battery?:** Yes
> **Charge time:** 3.5 hours
> **Weight:** 105 kg (231 lb)
> **Price:** $4,100-$5,000 in EU (varies by market)

NIU currently offers three lines of electric scooters, the N, M and U series. The N series is the most powerful, with the NGT serving as the flagship model. The NGT can reach speeds of 70 km/h (43.5 mph) with its 3 kW Bosch motor and 60 VDC system. One or two 2.1 kWh batteries can be used in the scooter. At 14 kg (31 lb), the batteries aren't light, but are still removable for convenient off-scooter charging. That high capacity gives the NGT the greatest range of all NIU scooters.

The NGT offers front and rear hydraulic suspension, a combined hydraulic braking system, a dynamic color display that changes color based on riding mode, auto-off turn signals and a cloud-connected controller with telematics reporting vehicle diagnostics from 32 sensors. The NGT also features a 3-axis movement detection alarm, three-mode positioning system (GPS, GLONASS and BEIDOU) for locating your scooter and GPS theft protection.

NIU also offers the NPro which is identical to the NGT except for its top speed which is limited to 45 km/h (28 mph). This allows it to qualify as a lower restriction/class vehicle in many countries.

# NIU M+                    NIU UPro

The M series is a slightly smaller and less powerful line of electric scooters. The M+ is the newest model in the M series and offers a lower top speed of 45 km/h (28 mph). Its 1.2 kW motor is not as sporty as the NGT, but still offers sufficient power to carry a passenger. The display is a large LCD screen situated between easy-to-use controls. The front and rear hydraulic brakes and hydraulic suspension give the scooter a comfortable ride and quick stopping. The M+ features similar LED lights and auto-off turn signals as the NGT. On-board GPS and the smartphone app also provide many of the same smart features such as lost vehicle locating, GPS anti-theft protection and 3-axis motion sensing.

The U line includes the smallest scooters offered by NIU. Built on an exposed steel frame, the scooters are designed for a single rider. The small motor is appropriate for the lower speed of these scooters, which are more like a step up from an electric bicycle. In fact, the UM scooter features pedals, turning it into a moped. The UPro has a similar design, but lacks the pedals of the UM and instead offers a slightly higher top speed.

**NIU M+**
**Motor power:** 1.2 kW (1.6 hp) continuous
                1.8 kW (2.4 hp) peak
**Torque:** 40 Nm (29.4 lb-ft)
**Top speed:** 45 km/h (28 mph)
**Range:** 100 km (62 mi) in ECO mode
**Acceleration:** 0-30 km/h (0-19 mph) in 4.5 seconds
**Battery capacity:** 2 kWh
**Removable battery?:** Yes
**Charge time:** 3.5 hours
**Weight:** 70 kg (154 lb)
**Price:** ~$2,900 in EU (varies by market)

**NIU UPro**
**Motor power:** 1.2 kW (1.6 hp) continuous
**Torque:** 24 Nm (17.6 lb-ft)
**Top speed:** 45 km/h (28 mph)
**Range:** 35 km (22 mi)
**Acceleration:** Not published
**Battery capacity:** 1 kWh
**Removable battery?:** Yes
**Charge time:** 4.5 hours
**Weight:** 55 kg (121 lb)
**Price:** ~$2,100 in EU (varies by market)

# GenZe 2.0s and 2.0f

GenZe is owned by Indian automotive giant Mahindra, but actually manufactures the GenZe 2.0 electric scooter in the US. Currently, these could be the only US-built electric scooters.

**GenZe 2.0s and 2.0f**
**Motor power:** 1.5 kW (2 hp)
**Torque:** 100 Nm (73 lb-ft)
**Top speed:** 48 km/h (30 mph)
**Range:** 48 km (30 mi)
**Acceleration:** 0-48 km/h (0-30 mph)
in 10 seconds
**Battery capacity:** 1.6 kWh
**Removable battery?:** Yes
**Charge time:** 4 hours
**Weight:** 105 kg (232 lb)
**Price:** $3,700-$4,200

The GenZe 2.0 is a well-designed urban commuter scooter. The 2.0s has a large cargo area behind the seat that functions like a pickup bed. A rider can easily toss cargo into the back and ride off. The courier model (2.0f) has a covered box that turns the rear bed into an enclosed, locking cargo box. The box can fit around 3 bags of groceries, depending on how good the rider is at stacking. It can easily fit a full face helmet and other gear, but struggles to fit two full face helmets and still close.

Speaking of two helmets, this is actually designed as a one person scooter, though does have enough power to carry a passenger on flat or moderately sloped ground. There are no foot pegs though, so it is best ridden solo.

The removable battery is excellently designed. It is positioned as low as possible on the scooter while still being easy to access and remove. At 13.6 kg (30 lb), the battery is not light but remains manageable. Part of that weight comes from the built-in 500 W charger. There's no need to remember the charger, as the rider simply plugs in a C13 cable (the type that computer power supplies use) and the battery begins charging. The charger is also fanless ,which results in silent charging.

The 7-inch color touchscreen shows a large analog-style speed readout and has equally large turn signal indicators that help remind the rider when the turn signals are active. The touchscreen is also used to unlock the scooter with a PIN code, no keys required.

The 2.0s has a single side stand, while the 2.0f comes with a locking center stand. When locked, the scooter can't be moved until the PIN code is entered.

The accompanying smartphone app uses telematics to allow a rider to remotely monitor the scooter, checking charge level, location, diagnostics and trip histories. GPS anti-theft and motion alerts help secure the scooter while it is parked.

# Etergo AppScooter

The AppScooter is one of the most high tech electric scooters on the market. Manufactured by Dutch scooter startup Etergo, the AppScooter is designed to be a convenient, long range electric scooter with a variety of connected features.

The large color screen integrates with a smartphone to provide alerts directly on the screen, preventing the rider from pulling out a phone while riding. It also offers GPS navigation directly on the screen, which minimizes other riding info like speed and battery life, but does not completely remove them from view. Buttons on the handlebars allow riders to navigate menus without taking their hands off the bars.

A centrally mounted AC motor uses a belt drive to transfer power to the rear wheel. Despite having a mid-mounted motor instead of a hub motor, there is still plenty of room for up to 3.47 kWh of battery. This is due to an ingenious battery design, with up to three banana-shaped modules that can be slid into a recess under the footwell. That not only lowers the center of gravity of the scooter, but also frees up the under seat cargo area to offer 60 L (2.11 cubic feet) of storage space.

**Etergo AppScooter**
**Motor power:** 3 kW (4 hp) continuous
6 kW (8 hp) peak
**Torque:** 135 Nm (99 lb-ft)
**Top speed:** 45 km/h (28 mph)
**Range:** 80-240 km (50-150 mi) with 1-3 batteries
at 20 km/h (12 mph)
**Acceleration:** 0-45 km/h (0-28 mph)
in 3.9 seconds
**Battery capacity:** 1.16 kWh per battery
up to 3.47 kWh with 3 batteries
**Removable battery?:** Yes
**Charge time:** 2.5-8 hours (depending on charger
and number of batteries)
**Weight:** 81.5 kg (180 lb) with one battery
**Price:** ~$3,900+ with 1 battery

Etergo is currently preparing to begin production of the AppScooter and expects to begin deliveries to reservation holders in the second half of 2019.

# BMW C Evolution

The BMW C Evolution is a powerful maxiscooter that sits halfway between an electric scooter and an electric motorcycle. It is undeniably a scooter, yet packs enough power and acceleration to feel nearly as sporty as a light motorbike. Its acceleration actually matches that of BMW's i3 electric car, which shares the same battery cells as the C Evolution.

**BMW C Evolution**
**Motor power:** 35 kW (48 hp)
**Torque:** 72 Nm (53 lb-ft)
**Top speed:** 129 km/h (80 mph)
**Range:** 159 km (99 mi)
**Acceleration:** 0-48 km/h (0-30 mph)
              in 2.8 seconds
**Battery capacity:** 12.69 kWh
**Removable battery?:** No
**Charge time:** 4.5 hours at 220 VAC (Level 2)
              9.3 hours at 110 VAC (Level 1)
**Weight:** 275 kg (606 lb)
**Price:** $13,750-$18,200 (varies by market)

The C Evolution features a bright TFT display that is easy to read, even in bright daylight. The display indicates speed, distance, time, trip info, odometer, range, riding mode and more. There are four riding modes, each with their unique characteristics. Dynamic Mode engages regenerative braking while coasting. Sail Mode allows the scooter to coast without any regenerative braking. Road Mode provides slightly relaxed acceleration and only moderate regenerative braking. Eco Pro Mode is designed to maximize battery by limiting power ramping and limiting the top speed to just 105 km/h (65 mph).

The C Evolution is quite heavy, but that weight is typically only noticeable when leaning the scooter while at rest. Otherwise, it tends to handle like a lighter scooter when cruising. The longer wheelbase keeps the C Evolution feeling stable at higher speeds, and built-in traction control adds confidence to the ride. The scooter's dual two piston hydraulic disc brakes in the front and single two piston hydraulic disc brake in the rear provide more than ample stopping power. The inverted hydraulic fork and rear mono shock create a responsive and comfortable ride.

For those that need a highway capable electric scooter that can easily carry a passenger or loads of cargo, and have the money to spare, the C Evolution is an excellent choice. With just 159 km (99 mi) of range, it is still limited to mostly urban and suburban outings, but that should be plenty for most riders.

# Vespa Elettrica

Relative to its specs, Vespa's Elettrica scooter is one of the most expensive electric scooters available. The Elettrica's 50 km/h (31 mph) top speed limits it to city riding, a setting where any Vespa should feel right at home.

The scooter packs an impressive range though, thanks to its large 4.2 kWh battery pack. Despite having impressive battery capacity and an on-board charger, the 25 kg (55 lb) battery is not removable. Instead, a charging cable is hidden under the seat that can connect to a wall outlet or a public charging station. That means riders will be limited to charging anywhere an extension cord can reach. For those living on the top floor of an apartment building, the Elettrica might not be the most appropriate choice for an electric scooter.

**Vespa Elettrica**
**Motor power:** 3.5 kW (4.7 hp) continuous
4 kW (5.4 hp) peak
**Torque:** 200 Nm (148 lb-ft)
**Top speed:** 50 km/h (31 mph)
**Range:** 100 km (60 mi) in ECO mode at 29 km/h (18 mph)
**Acceleration:** Not published
**Battery capacity:** 4.2 kWh
**Removable battery?:** No
**Charge time:** 4 hours with 220 VAC
**Weight:** 130 kg (287 lb)
**Price:** ~$7,499 (varies by market)

The Elettrica pays homage to classic Vespa styling with its monocoque construction. The single-sided rear swingarm and single-sided front monoshock strut help retain the classic look of standard Vespa wheels. The bike features a front disc brake and rear drum brake.

Vespa did include a number of high tech features in the Elettrica. The 4.3-inch color touchscreen display uses an ambient light sensor to constantly adjust brightness and optimize visibility. The display can also be used in conjunction with the rider's smartphone. Handlebar controls allow the rider to perform functions such as answering calls, checking notifications, managing music and activating voice commands.

The Vespa Elettrica certainly wins accolades in the design department, but its price may keep it out of reach for many who seek an economical scooter.

# Flux Mopeds EM1

The Flux EM1 was designed by Flux Mopeds in Wisconsin and is produced in China. While most city scooters available in the US are limited to a maximum speed of 48 km/h (30 mph), the EM1 has a higher top speed of 61 km/h (38 mph). However, this means that it might require more than just a standard driver's license in some US states.

**Flux Mopeds EM1**
**Motor power:** 1.5 kW (2 hp)
**Torque:** Not published
**Top speed:** 61 km/h (38 mph)
**Range:** 80 km (50 mi) with 2 batteries
**Acceleration:** 0-48 km/h (0-30 mph) in 8 seconds
**Battery capacity:** 1.44 kWh per battery
2.88 kWh with 2 batteries
**Removable battery?:** Yes
**Charge time:** 3 hours with 110 VAC
**Weight:** 73 kg (160 lb) empty
92.5 kg (204 lb) with 2 batteries
**Price:** $2,399

The EM1 can be used with either one or two batteries held in the under seat compartment. The scooter uses independent hydraulic disc brakes in the front and rear. Suspension is accomplished with a telescopic front fork and dual rear coilover suspension.

While many budget-level electric scooters in the US are simply rebranded imports, Flux worked with their factory to develop the majority of the EM1's design in-house, making it exclusive to this scooter.

The scooter features modest acceleration and limited features. There is no smartphone connectivity, color screen or GPS tracking. However, the EM1's price sets it apart in the US as one of the most affordable electric scooters available. For anyone seeking an affordable, reliable yet spartan electric scooter, the EM1 from Flux Mopeds would make an excellent choice.

# UJET

The UJET scooter, developed in Luxembourg, is the epitome of a luxury electric city scooter. While the price seems quite high (and it is), the UJET can do something no other electric scooter can: fold elegantly.

The UJET can fold into a small dolly that can be wheeled around easily. A rider could realistically commute around town on the UJET all day, then arrive home to fold the scooter and bring it up to their penthouse apartment in the elevator.

The battery compartment is also the seat, and the two disconnect from the scooter to allow for charging away from the scooter. But instead of carrying the battery, the rider can simply wheel it around like a rolling carry-on suitcase using its built in wheels and telescopic handle.

In addition to the novel folding mechanism, the UJET sports a unique design. Both of its 14" wheels are hubless and supported by single sided armatures. The wheels have three points of contact and use inverted disc brakes. The large diameter discs and hydraulic brake pistons ensure powerful stopping.

> **UJET**
> **Motor power:** 1.75 kW (2.3 hp) continuous
> 3.6 kW (4.8 hp) peak
> **Torque:** 80 Nm (58.8 lb-ft)
> **Top speed:** 45 km/h (28 mph)
> **Range:** 35-75 km (21-47 mi) on 1.2 kWh
> 75-150 km (47-93 mi) on 2.4 kWh
> **Acceleration:** Not published
> **Battery capacity:** 1.2 kWh or 2.4 kWh options
> **Removable battery?:** Yes
> **Charge time:** 1.5-3 hours with external fast charger
> 3-6 hours with on-board charger
> **Weight:** 49 kg (108 lb) with 1.2 kWh battery
> 55 kg (121 lb) with 2.4 kWh battery
> **Price:** $8,100-$10,000 (varies by market and VAT)

The UJET features an automatically folding 7-inch color TFT display that includes phone pairing for turn-by-turn navigation, music, notifications, GPS tracking and anti-theft protection. The UJET also includes a front-facing video camera. The UJET smartphone app allows riders to unlock the scooter with their phones and share the scooter with contacts. Users can also keep their phone and other devices charged with the scooter's two USB ports.

The UJET is an expensive premium scooter designed for luxury customers. But unlike some scooters with high price tags, the UJET actually delivers premium design and functionality for its price.

# Zapp i300

The Zapp i300 is a high performance electric scooter designed to offer the performance of a light electric motorcycle with the style and convenience of a scooter. With a high power motor and powerful acceleration, the Zapp i300 targets sportier users seeking a thrilling ride.

**Zapp i300**
**Motor power:** 14 kW (18.8 hp)
**Torque:** 587 Nm (432 lb-ft) at rear wheel
**Top speed:** 97 km/h (60 mph)
**Range:** 56 km (35 mi) in ECO mode with 2 batteries
**Acceleration:** 0-48 km/h (0-30 mph) in 2.3 seconds
                  0-72 km/h (0-45 mph) in 4.1 seconds
**Battery capacity:** 2x 1.25 kWh (2.5 kWh total)
**Removable battery?:** Yes
**Charge time:** 4 hours
**Weight:** 90 kg (198 lb)
**Price:** ~$7,150

Don't expect that ride to last long though - as the scooter can only reach a maximum range of 56 km (35 mi) in ECO mode under ideal conditions. The range at full speed is expected to be much less.

The low range is due to the combination of modest battery capacity and a high power motor. The batteries are slim, 2 inch (5 cm) thick units that look sleek and modern but provide limited capacity. Combined with such a high power motor, they simply don't provide much usable range at high speeds.

The structural aluminum body covers a steel tube frame that supports a single-sided rear swingarm and a telescopic front fork. Anti-lock full floating hydraulic disc brakes provide plenty of stopping power to counteract the 14 kW belt drive motor. A high resolution color display provides the scooter's speed, riding mode, battery charge, temperature, range and other important parameters.

First deliveries of the Zapp i300 are expected to begin in the Q2 2019.

# OjO Electric Scooter

The OjO electric scooter was designed by a Santa Monica startup as a small, nimble urban scooter. However, its limited range and speed place it closer to an electric bicycle than most larger electric scooters and mopeds. The OjO does excel as a bike lane vehicle for navigating crowded urban centers.

The small wheels don't do the ride quality any favors, but rear swingarm suspension and a front monoshock fork help to smooth out the ride. The rear hub motor frees up room under the floorboard for a removable battery. An onboard charger is built into the OjO scooter and includes a retractable charging cord in the front of the scooter.

Mechanical disc brakes are sufficient for the relatively low 32 km/h (20 mph) top speed. The scooter is so small and narrow that riders can easily put their feet out if they feel unstable. This can help new riders feel more confident, as the limited speed and power means the scooter is unlikely to get away from them. The scooter is also built for larger riders in mind, featuring a weight capacity of 136 kg (300 lb).

**OjO Electric Scooter**
**Motor power:** 500 W
**Torque:** 100 Nm (73.5 lb-ft)
**Top speed:** 32 km/h (20 mph)
**Range:** 40 km (25 mi)
**Acceleration:** Not published
**Battery capacity:** 720 Wh
**Removable battery?:** Yes
**Charge time:** 6-8 hours
**Weight:** 31.8 kg (70 lb)
**Price:** $2,000-$2,400 (varies by model)

The display includes a large touchscreen that clearly displays speed, range, battery capacity and other useful parameters. It also indicates which of three different riding modes is selected and offers Bluetooth integration with smartphones. The scooter can play music from a rider's smartphone via its dual waterproof speakers and provide notifications of incoming calls on the display. There is also a USB port for charging devices during use.

A motion activated alarm and key fob locking system helps keep the scooter secure when parked. Without unlocking via the key fob, the scooter is immobilized.

OjO has multiple variations of their base model scooter, including a licensing agreement with Ford that adds a few accessories including mirrors.

While this level of performance can be found in many electric bicycles for a lower price, the OjO has an undeniably charming design that many find endearing and provides a nice "missing link" vehicle between e-bikes and e-scooters.

# Doohan iTank DB45          Doohan iTank DB70

The Chinese company Doohan manufactures several models of innovative three-wheeled leaning electric scooters. The iTank scooters have a tilting mechanism that allows them to lean up to 30º in either direction. The front wheels can also raise up independently to 183 mm (7 in), allowing riders to tackle uneven terrain or drops from street curbs.

The three-wheeled design is more stable than a typical two-wheeled scooter. It also allows the rider to keep his or her feet on the scooter at stops. The iTank includes three dual-piston hydraulic brakes resulting in a short stopping distance. Front and rear hydraulic suspension is also standard on the iTank.

The iTank is available in a lower speed version that offers one 1.56 kWh battery and a 1.49 kW Bosch motor or a higher speed version that requires two 1.56 kWh batteries feeding a 3 kW QS Motor.  The DB45 and DB70 are largely identical, with the sole difference being the DB70's higher speed when powered by two batteries.

The 9 kg (20 lb) batteries can be charged on the scooter or removed for charging indoors. The batteries are built using LG or Panasonic battery cells (depending on the market).

In addition to the iTank, Doohan also produces a lighter weight, three-wheeled leaning electric scooter called the iTango that has a lower power motor and is limited to a maximum of 45 km/h (28 mph). Both are designed to carry up to two people and are rated for a maximum load of 160 kg (353 lb) for the iTank or 154 kg (340 lb) for the iTango. The iTango is typically priced at about $500 less than the iTank.

**Doohan iTank DB45**
**Motor power:** 1.49 kW (2 hp)
**Torque:** 128 Nm (94 lb-ft)
**Top speed:** 45 km/h (28 mph)
**Range:** 45 km (28 mi) at 45 km/h (28 mph)
**Acceleration:** Not published
**Battery capacity:** 1.56 kWh
**Removable battery?:** Yes
**Charge time:** 7-8 hours
**Weight:** 100 kg (220 lb)
**Price:** $3,300 - $3,500 (varies by market)

**Doohan iTank DB70**
**Motor power:** 3 kW (4 hp)
**Torque:** 150 Nm (110 lb-ft)
**Top speed:** 70 km/h (43.5 mph)
**Range:** 60 km (37 mi) at 70 km/h (43.5 mph)
**Acceleration:** 0-45 km/h (0-28 mph) in 4.6 seconds
**Battery capacity:** 3.12 kWh (2x 1.56 kWh)
**Removable battery?:** Yes
**Charge time:** 5-8 hours (varies by charger option)
**Weight:** 100 kg (220 lb)
**Price:** $3,900 - $4,630 (varies by market)

# Torrot Muvi City      Torrot Muvi Executive

The Torrot Muvi line of scooters are produced in Spain and offer a lower speed (City) and higher speed (Executive) option. Both scooters have tubular steel frames, single side-mounted rear monoshocks, front hydraulic telescoping forks, 16" wheels and combined hydraulic disc brakes. Both models also use a drive belt to transfer power from the mid-mounted motor to the rear wheel. The models basically differ in speed and power ratings.

The large wheels offer an improved ride over potholes and road debris, but also make the Muvi less nimble than many scooters with smaller wheels. The 4-inch LCD display is not as impressive as the colorful LED screens found on other scooters but is clearly visible in all lighting conditions and easy to read. The display's design is customizable with different themes by connecting to a smartphone app via Bluetooth and GSM. The factory can also provide over-the-air updates to the scooter via GSM.

The Muvi is relatively light by electric scooter standards, even with the optional second battery. This makes it great for beginners, and is perhaps one reason it is often used in scooter sharing programs. The scooter's acceleration is rather unimpressive, though this helps contribute to better range in urban settings, especially in stop-and-go traffic.

**Torrot Muvi City**
**Motor power:** 2.65 kW (3.6 hp)
**Torque:** Not published
**Top speed:** 45 km/h (28 mph)
**Range:** 45 km (28 mi) with 1 battery (can be doubled with 2 batteries)
**Acceleration:** 0-30 km/h (0-22 mph) in 8.5 seconds
**Battery capacity:** 1.62 kWh, option of 3.24 kWh with 2 batteries
**Removable battery?:** Yes
**Charge time:** 5 hours (standard charger) or 2.5 hours (fast charger)
**Weight:** 85 kg (187 lb)
**Price:** $3,600-$5,000 (varies by market and taxes)

**Torrot Muvi Executive**
**Motor power:** 3 kW (4 hp)
**Torque:** Not published
**Top speed:** 60 km/h (37 mph)
**Range:** 40 km (25 mi) with 1 battery (can be doubled with 2 batteries)
**Acceleration:** Not published
**Battery capacity:** 1.62 kWh, option of 3.24 kWh with 2 batteries
**Removable battery?:** Yes
**Charge time:** 5 hours (standard charger) or 2.5 hours (fast charger)
**Weight:** 85 kg (187 lb)
**Price:** $3,850-$5,100 (varies by market and taxes)

# Kumpan 1954Ri S    Kumpan 1954Ri    Kumpan 1953

Kumpan is a German scooter manufacturer that produces high quality, retro-inspired electric scooters. A casual observer will notice their similarity to Vespa's iconic design. In fact, Vespa has taken legal action against Kumpan, alleging that the design copies Vespa's. Nonetheless, Kumpan's models offer performance and convenience that Vespa's own Elettrica scooter has yet to achieve.

The most powerful scooter in the lineup is the 1954 Ri S, which can reach speeds of 100 km/h (62 mph). The 1954 Ri is nearly identical except for a lower power motor and lower top speed of 45 km/h (28 mph). Both scooters feature high-end accoutrements including a beautifully designed 7-inch color touch screen interface, keyless start, cruise control, hidden cup holder, small storage compartment between the rider's feet and sharp LED lighting. Hydraulic disc brakes with anti-lock braking provide quick stopping while hydraulic suspension results in a comfortable ride.

Both models come with one or two batteries, but can accept a third. Each battery conveniently drops into a slot under the seat and includes a digital readout.

Kumpan's third electric scooter is the smaller 1953. With just a 2.5 kW motor, it doesn't offer the same powerful acceleration but is still plenty capable for urban commuting. It does lack passenger foot pegs though, so is better used as a single rider scooter. The 1953 model does not have the same luxurious feel as the 1954 Ri models, but does feature a convenient utility rack. It is also much more affordable, which could win over many budget-minded riders.

**Kumpan 1954Ri S**
**Motor power:** 7 kW (9.4 hp)
**Torque:** Not published
**Top speed:** 100 km/h (62 mph)
**Range:** 80 km (50 mi) with 2 batteries
          120 km (75 mi) with 3 batteries
**Acceleration:** Not published
**Battery capacity:** 2.96 kWh with 2 batteries
                     4.44 kWh with 3 batteries
**Removable battery?:** Yes
**Charge time:** 3 hours per battery
**Weight:** 100 kg (220 lb) with 2 batteries
**Price:** ~$7,900 with single battery (varies by market)

**Kumpan 1954Ri**
**Motor power:** 4 kW (5.4 hp)
**Torque:** Not published
**Top speed:** 45 km/h (28 mph)
**Range:** 60 km (37 mi) with 1 battery
          180 km (112 mi) with 3 batteries
**Acceleration:** Not published
**Battery capacity:** 1.48 kWh with 1 battery
                     4.44 kWh with 3 batteries
**Removable battery?:** Yes
**Charge time:** 3 hours per battery
**Weight:** 100 kg (220 lb) with 2 batteries
**Price:** ~$5,700 with single battery (varies by market)

**Kumpan 1953**
**Motor power:** 2.5 kW (3.4 hp)
**Torque:** 100 Nm (73.5 lb-ft)
**Top speed:** 45 km/h (28 mph)
**Range:** 50 km (30 mi) with 1 battery
          150 km (90 mi) with 3 batteries
**Acceleration:** Not published
**Battery capacity:** 1.48 kWh per battery
**Removable battery?:** Yes
**Charge time:** 3-4 hours per battery
**Weight:** 74.5 kg (164 lb) with 1 battery
**Price:** ~$4,350 (varies by market)

# Govecs Schwalbe L1E       Govecs Schwalbe L3E

The Govecs Schwalbe electric scooter is a modern day take on the classic East German Schwalbe scooter. Two versions are currently available, differing in power and speed. With its retro styling, the new Schwalbe certainly looks the part of a classic scooter.

The Schwalbe uses a suite of Bosch parts including motor, batteries, on-board charger and 4.4" LCD display. The motor uses a belt primary and secondary reduction for quiet operation. The 1.2 kW charger includes a 5 M (16 ft) coiled power cord hidden under the seat. Due to their size, the 2.4 kWh batteries are not removable, and therefore the on-board charger is a necessity.

Belying its vintage aesthetic are a number of high tech components. Both models of the scooter offer regenerative braking, a connected smartphone app, USB charging, 5 L of under seat storage and hydraulic disc brakes. The faster L3E model includes a combined braking system and both models offer anti-lock brakes as an optional upgrade.

While the L1e model is limited to city use, the L3e scooter is quick enough for higher speed roads, opening up additional possibilities for riders.

**Govecs Schwalbe L3E**
**Motor power:** 8 kW (10.7 hp)
**Torque:** Not published
**Top speed:** 90 km/h (56 mph)
**Range:** 90 km (56 mi)
**Acceleration:** Not published
**Battery capacity:** 4.8 kWh (divided into 2x 2.4 kWh packs)
**Removable battery?:** No
**Charge time:** 4.75 hours
**Weight:** 135 kg (298 lb)
**Price:** ~$8,000 (varies by market and options)

**Govecs Schwalbe L1E**
**Motor power:** 4 kW (5.4 hp)
**Torque:** Not published
**Top speed:** 45 km/h (28 mph)
**Range:** 60 km (37 mi) with 1 battery
      120 km (74 mi) with 2 batteries
**Acceleration:** Not published
**Battery capacity:** 2.4 kWh (or 4.8 kWh with optional second battery)
**Removable battery?:** No
**Charge time:** 4.5 hours
**Weight:** 120 kg (265 lb) with 1 battery
      135 kg (298 lb) with 2 batteries
**Price:** ~$6,100 (varies by market and options)

# Silence S01

Silence is a Spanish electric scooter manufacturer that began by building electric scooters for commercial use. The scooters became popular for use by delivery companies and for municipal operations, including police and first responders.

**Silence S01**
**Motor power:** 6 kW (8 hp) continuous, 11 kW
               (14.75 hp) peak
**Torque:** Not published
**Top speed:** 100 km/h (62 mph)
**Range:** 115 km (71 mi)
**Acceleration:** 0-50 km/h (0-31 mph) in 3.8 seconds
**Battery capacity:** 5 kWh
**Removable battery?:** Yes
**Charge time:** 6 hours for full charge
               3-4 hours for 70%
**Weight:** 135 kg (298 lb)
**Price:** $6,800 - $7,400 (varies by market)

2019 marked the beginning of Silence's consumer operations when they debuted the S01 and began taking pre-orders. Though the scooter was originally only sold in Spain, Silence began expand the S01's availability throughout Europe in April 2019.

The S01 uses Silence's innovative trolley battery design. Most electric scooters struggle to pack more than 2 kWh of capacity into a removable battery before it becomes too heavy to easily handle. While some scooters employ multiple batteries, it can still be difficult to juggle the total weight. Silence uses a single large battery with built-in wheels and an extendable handle that allows it to be rolled like carry-on luggage. The battery pack is released with a simple latch under the seat, then can be slid sideways out of the scooter. The wheels automatically drop down as the battery is slide out. The entire design is rather ingenious and helps to provide the S01 with both long range and convenient charging.

A 600 W charger with recoiling cord is built into the battery to make charging as convenient as possible. An integral heater is also included in the battery to keep the pack warm and prevent damage during cold weather charging.

Battery innovations aside, the S01 is an impressive scooter in its own right. The powerful 6 kW motor peaks at 11 kW to provide ample acceleration. The top speed of 100 km/h (62 mph) creates more freedom of road choice, whether on urban streets or country highways. The long range of the large capacity battery means that higher speeds don't reduce the real-world range to an undesirably small amount.

The wide seat comfortably fits two riders without crowding and leaves enough room under the seat for two helmets. The seat can even be opened remotely via the connected smartphone app, which can also be used to turn on the scooter. The app displays the scooter's historical and current data. Both the scooter and the battery have built-in GPS, allowing them to be tracked if either is stolen. The scooter has hydraulic suspension, hydraulic disc brakes with a combined braking system and regenerative braking.

The S01 certainly isn't the least expensive electric scooter in Europe, not by a long shot. But compared to other scooters in its price range, it has the one of the best engineered battery systems plus greater range and more power, making the S01 a clear favorite.

# Unu

Unu is a German company that manufactures its scooters in China for the European market. Their scooter is available with three different power levels of 1 kW, 2 kW and 3 kW. All three have the same range and top speed, though the higher power models are available with more color options and are less sluggish on hills.

Unu scooters are designed to be ultra-affordable and, as a result, performance isn't overwhelming. The Bosch motors are high quality, but the controllers limit power to a quite modest level in order to optimize battery life and range. The result is slower acceleration than most other electric scooters.

Despite the slower acceleration and reduced power, the scooters themselves are otherwise quite respectable. They come with a single battery, but can support two, effectively doubling the range. The batteries are housed in an attractive brushed aluminum case and come with a carry strap for easy transport. The seat fits two riders, though with a second rider the scooter's performance will drop. The chrome mirrors and speedometer housing certainly add to the chic style of the little scooter. That speedometer is analog, a rare sight on electric scooters these days. Instead of overwhelming the rider with data like many other scooter digital displays, the Unu's minimalist display houses just two classic analog needles pointing out speed and battery level. Simple and elegant.

> **Unu**
> **Motor power:** 1 kW / 2 kW / 3 kW (1.3 hp / 2.7 hp / 4 hp)
> **Torque:** Not published
> **Top speed:** 45 km/h (28 mph)
> **Range:** 50 km (31 mi) with 1 battery (can be doubled with second battery)
> **Acceleration:** 0-45 km/h (0-28 mph) 1 kW - 17 seconds; 2 kW - 14 seconds; 3 kW - 12 seconds
> **Battery capacity:** 1.44 kWh
> **Removable battery?:** Yes
> **Charge time:** 5 hours, or 70% in 2 hours
> **Weight:** 66 kg (146 lb) with 1 battery
> **Price:** 1 kW ~$2,000; 2 kW ~$2,600; 3 kW ~$3,150

Braking comes from a hydraulic disc brake in the front and a combination of a mechanical drum brake and regenerative braking in the rear. Even with all three working in tandem on the lightweight Unu, the braking distance isn't quite as good as other scooters.

Unu Scooters aren't available in standard stores or dealerships. Riders must customize and order their scooter online after taking a test ride with local sales representatives known as "Pioneers". With over 10,000 Unu scooters on the streets of Europe, the unique sales approach certainly appears to be working well for the company.

# Vostok E7

Vostok is a new Spanish company with a novel electric scooter designed for the European market and manufactured in China. The scooters are fairly low power with limited performance, but offered at a lower price than nearly any other electric scooter in Europe.

**Vostok E7**
**Motor power:** 2.25 kW (3 hp)
**Torque:** Not published
**Top speed:** 45 km/h (28 mph)
**Range:** 75 km (47 mi) with 1 battery, can double with 2 batteries
**Acceleration:** Not published
**Battery capacity:** 1.56 kWh (option for 3.12 kWh with 2 batteries)
**Removable battery?:** Yes
**Charge time:** 3 hours
**Weight**: 90 kg (198 lb) without battery
**Price:** MSRP ~$2,150, presale price ~$1,850

The scooters can support one or two removable 60 V batteries. Each battery can be recharged in three hours with a standard 220 VAC outlet. Brakes include front hydraulic disc brakes and a rear drum brake along with regenerative braking via the rear hub motor.

The Vostok scooter includes an independent second rear seat that can carry a passenger or cargo. The handlebars support a fairly simple LCD display that includes standard readouts including speed, distance and battery charge level. The display also shows a power bar along the bottom of the screen that helps a rider learn to better control their energy usage. The Vostok E7 includes a wireless key fob that unlocks the scooter and sets an anti-theft alarm.

Vostok doesn't offer the range of features seen in other electric scooters. You'll notice the absence of any GPS, GSM or Bluetooth connectivity and accompanying smartphone app. The Vostok E7 is purely a simple scooter designed to be an effective city commuter at a reasonable price, a goal that it appears to have achieved. Riders that require more features should look elsewhere, as this is a scooter intended to be utilitarian and affordable. Think Model T, but for electric scooters. Simple, effective and easy on the wallet.

# Ather S340                                    Ather 450

Ather Energy produces what many riders consider to be the best electric scooters in India. The Ather S340 and higher power Ather 450 are both high tech smart scooters with excellent performance characteristics.

The scooters feature 7" capacitive touch LCD screens. Users can create an on-board, password-protected profile with custom performance settings. In addition to standard riding data, such as speed and battery charge level, the display provides turn-by-turn GPS navigation and connects with a smartphone to show alerts and calls.

The scooters employ a nearly silent two-stage belt reduction that provides high torque to the rear wheel. Braking includes front and rear hydraulic disc brakes with a combined braking system. A telescopic front fork and rear hydraulic monoshock comprise the suspension.

Ather Energy is currently working on developing a network of charging stations that can provide fast charging. Riders can also charge from a home charging point or carry an AC charger for charging on the go. The battery packs are not removable, meaning riders will need to park close enough to an outlet or bring an extension cord.

| **Ather S340** | **Ather 450** |
|---|---|
| **Motor power:** 2.8 kW (3.8 hp) continuous<br>4.4 kW (5.9 hp) peak | **Motor power:** 3.3 kW (4.4 hp) continuous<br>5.4 kW (7.2 hp) peak |
| **Torque:** 20 Nm (14.7 lb-ft) | **Torque:** 20.5 Nm (15.1 lb-ft) |
| **Top speed:** 70 km/h (44 mph) | **Top speed:** 80 km/h (50 mph) |
| **Range:** 60 km (37 mi) in Eco mode<br>50 km (31 mi) in Sport mode | **Range:** 75 km (47 mi) in Eco mode<br>60 km (37 mi) in Sport mode |
| **Acceleration:** 0-40 km/h (0-25 mph) in 5.1 seconds | **Acceleration:** 0-40 km/h (0-25 mph) in 3.9 seconds |
| **Battery capacity:** 1.92 kWh | **Battery capacity:** 2.4 kWh |
| **Removable battery?:** No | **Removable battery?:** No |
| **Charge time:** 4.3 hours on Level 1<br>fast charging at 1 km/min | **Charge time:** 4.3 hours on Level 1<br>fast charging at 1 km/min |
| **Weight:** 118 kg (260 lb) | **Weight:** 118 kg (260 lb) |
| **Price:** ~$1,580 | **Price:** ~$1,800 |

# Okinawa i-Praise      Okinawa Ridge+

Okinawa Scooters produces a number of lower power electric scooters for the Indian market. The i-Praise and Ridge+ are the company's newest models and will begin deliveries in early 2019. Despite the i-Praise's low power, it is one of the fastest electric scooters currently available in India. It will just require some time to get up to speed.

Despite the Ridge+ claiming a 100 km range, riders have reported that the 1.75 kWh battery is only capable of between 60-80 km in most cases. The i-Praise will begin deliveries later this year, and therefore it remains to be seen if its battery will be similarly overrated.

The i-Praise and Ridge+ both feature GPS tracking and a "Find My Scooter" function as well geo-fencing and remote immobilization as anti-theft features. The on-board computer offers maintenance and insurance reminders, battery health information and speed alerts. However, the scooters have rather simple LCD screens compared to the higher quality screens found on some of their local competitors.

The Ridge+ and i-Praise have front hydraulic telescopic forks and dual rear shocks to smooth out some of the notoriously bumpy local roads. Hydraulic disc brakes are aided by regenerative braking. The seat fits two riders and leaves 7 L of storage space in the i-Praise and 17 L of storage in the Ridge+.

Both models are the first offered by Okinawa with removable batteries and were intended to make charging more convenient. Removable scooter batteries are comparatively less common in India.

Okinawa also offers versions of both scooters that are powered by SLA batteries that reduce their ranges.

| Okinawa i-Praise | Okinawa Ridge+ |
|---|---|
| **Motor power:** 1 kW (1.3 hp) continuous 2.5 kW (3.4 hp) peak | **Motor power:** 0.8 kW (1.07 hp) continuous 1.2 kW (1.6 hp) peak |
| **Torque:** Not published | **Torque:** Not published |
| **Top speed:** 75 km/h (47 mph) | **Top speed:** 55 km/h (34 mph) |
| **Range:** 160 km (99 mi) in Eco mode at 35 km/h (22 mph) | **Range:** 100 km (62 mi) in Eco mode |
| **Acceleration:** Not published | **Acceleration:** Not published |
| **Battery capacity:** 2.9 kWh | **Battery capacity:** 1.75 kWh |
| **Removable battery?:** Yes | **Removable battery?:** Yes |
| **Charge time:** 3 hours with high power 220 VAC wall charger | **Charge time:** 3 hours with high power charger 220 VAC wall charger |
| **Weight:** 150 kg (331 lb) | **Weight:** 96 kg (212 lb) |
| **Price:** ~$1,700 | **Price:** ~$1,075 |

# Coming Soon

The previous sections included a series of electric motorcycles and scooters that should be available for purchase at some point in 2019. In addition, there are a number of other electric two-wheelers that are nearing their own launches but aren't quite ready to be included in the main section of this book.

Some of these may still be available near the end of 2019, depending on the progress of the respective companies, but others aren't expected until at least 2020, if not later. However, there is enough known about the following bikes that it would be a shame not to include them in this book.

So while the following bikes might not be available yet, riders can expect to see them coming soon.

Novus electric motorcycle

# RMK E2

RMK is a Finnish company developing a unique electric motorcycle. The E2 uses an in-wheel motor as part of a hubless wheel. The novel design was developed in-house by the company. The motor is rated at 50 kW (67 hp) with 320 Nm (236 lb-ft) of torque. RMK says it should propel the E2 to 160 km/h (100 mph). The unique motor design is striking and saves room in the frame for a large battery pack. RMK hasn't yet revealed the size of the battery but indicate that the E2 should have a range of 200-300 km (120-180 mi). The bike also sports a digital interface built directly into the tank area, leaving the handlebars clean and uncluttered. The price is expected to be about $26,600. RMK is already accepting pre-orders but an estimated delivery date has not been announced.

# Tarform

Tarform is a New York based electric motorcycle startup with a fashionable cafe racer prototype. The motorcycle is an interesting mix of vintage cues and modern design. 3D printing was used to create a number of the more complicated body components. Each component from the louvered headlight to the hydraulic brake levers and reservoirs match the design aesthetic of the bike. The bike is still undergoing design changes but the company says its battery should be sufficient for 145 km (90 mi) in the city and 80 km (50 mi) on the highway. Charging time is expected to be 4 hours for a complete charge. Tarform is taking pre-orders for deliveries that are expected in late 2019 or early 2020. The cost is expected to be about $18,000.

# Curtiss

Curtiss Motorcycles, formerly Confederate Cycles, morphed into an electric-only motorcycle company in 2018 and has since rolled out a number of insanely high power concepts and prototypes. Their Zeus concept electric motorcycle has been refined into two different models, a bobber and a cafe racer. The original prototype used two Zero electric motorcycles coupled to a single drive shaft, resulting in 127 kW (170 hp) and 393 Nm (290 lb-ft) of torque. The more recent models have seen that power increase up to 140 kW (188 hp). The Zeus models aren't expected to reach the market until 2020 at the very earliest and there is no word yet on pricing. Don't expect them to come cheap.

# Ducati

Ducati has not yet revealed any details or specs on an electric motorcycle. However, the company's CEO Claudio Domenicali was quoted in January of 2019 as saying, "The future is electric, we're not far from starting series production". Domenicali has been optimistic about Ducati's entrance into the electric motorcycle market and those words indicate that the company has already begun development of at least one electric model. They could be planning to partner with an outside firm for the R&D process. Ducati did something similar in 2018 when it partnered with Thok E-bikes to develop and produce the Ducati Mig-RR electric mountain bike. So while there are no hard details on a Ducati electric motorcycle yet, we are expecting to hear good news soon.

# Novus

Novus is a new German electric motorcycle startup that unveiled their first model at CES 2019. The carbon fiber bike is the epitome of a light electric motorcycle. It weighs just 39 kg (85 lb) and has a top speed of 97 km/h (60 mph) with a rear wheel hub motor putting out a peak of 14 kW (18.8 hp). According to the company, that should be good for a 0-97 km/h (0-60 mph) time of 2.1 seconds. The bike is wild looking, but the astronomical price of $39,500, before VAT, will place it out of reach of most serious riders. The Novus is beautiful from just about every angle, but is still a true luxury bike that most people will never get to see or touch.

# Ural

The Russian sidecar motorcycle manufacturer Ural is known for a number of three-wheeled models. However, it took until 2018 for the company to begin playing with electric motors. As part of a partnership with Zero Motorcycles, Ural used a Zero drivetrain to convert their cT platform into an electric sidecar motorcycle. Zero provided engineering help to complete the project. But don't get too excited to hop in the sidecar just yet. Ural estimates that it will be a minimum of two years before the project can be ramped up to serial production after final design approval.

# KYMCO SuperNEX

KYMCO is best known as the largest scooter manufacturer in Taiwan. They entered the electric scooter market in the summer of 2018 with their Ionex line of electric scooters and swappable battery standard. KYMCO then shocked the motorcycle world in November of 2018 when they unveiled the SuperNEX at EICMA 2018 in Milan. The SuperNEX is the company's first electric motorcycle and is optimized for high speed racing as an electric supersport. It can go from 0-100 km/h (0-62 mph) in 2.9 seconds or 0-200 km/h (0-124 mph) in 7.5 seconds. It tops out at 250 km/h (155 mph). Even more interesting, KYMCO decided to outfit their bike with a 6-speed manual transmission, though with a slipper clutch to make shifting easier. There is no word yet on when the SuperNEX will be available for purchase or at what price.

# Arc Vector

Arc was founded by a group of former Jaguar engineers as an ultra-luxury electric motorcycle. With a price tag of $117,000, the Arc Vector is in a class all its own. While not the fastest electric motorcycle at a top speed of 200 km/h (125 mph), it certainly is quick off the line. Its 0-97 km/h (0-60 mph) time is 3.1 seconds. Range is estimated to be 193 km (120 mi) on the highway or 322 km (200 mi) in the city. The Arc Vector has a carbon fiber monocoque and swingarm, custom Öhlins suspension and Brembo brakes. It also comes with a special HUD helmet and haptic feedback jacket, both of which interface with the Vector to provide visual and physical cues to the rider. Only 399 units will be produced, making this bike not just expensive but also highly exclusive.

# Pursang

Pursang is a Barcelona-based electric motorcycle startup. The name Pursang comes from Bultaco's US-version gas motorcycle, originally introduced in 1965. The rebirth of an electric Pursang will come in two forms: the 6 kW E-Street and the 11 kW BigBore. The bikes are expected to have a top speed of 120 km/h (75 mph) and a maximum range of 100 km (62 mi) with two batteries manufactured by Torrot. Both bikes sport impressive designs and styling, marking a strong start for Pursang. The bikes are now available for pre-order reservations, but the company does not yet have an estimated delivery date.

# Honda PCX Electric

Honda's PCX Electric is technically already available, but the company is rolling the scooter out *very* slowly. It is nearly unobtainable and has only been produced in small numbers of less than a few hundred units, and is so far only available for lease in a few select areas. For that reason it is included in the Coming Soon section of this book. The PCX Electric features a 4.2 kW (5.7 hp) mid-motor. The scooter uses two of Honda's removable batteries that provide a combined range of 42 km (26 mi). The batteries are similar in form and function to Gogoro's and also use public battery swap stations.

# Honda EV-Cub

Honda has produced over 100 million units based on variations of its popular gas Super Cub scooter and motorbikes. The company has claimed to be working on an EV version at various times since 2009, and has recently indicated it could begin to roll out as soon as 2020. Concepts displayed by Honda have featured two-wheel drive with a hub motor in each wheel, a design rarely seen on production electric scooters and motorcycles. The concepts held true to the original vintage design aesthetics, while offering a modern and sleek look. However, there just isn't much info available yet on a possible EV-Cub. In the meantime, a company known as Shanghai Customs offers an interesting electric conversion kit that can turn vintage Honda Super Cubs into EVs. For now that's the closest that riders can get to an EV-Cub.

# NXT Rage

NXT Motors is a new Dutch startup electric motorcycle manufacturer. They have two naked bike prototypes currently in pre-production. NXT hasn't released performance specs yet, but are already taking order reservations. The NXT Rage features a carbon fiber monocoque, a large 7" color display and Öhlins suspension. The NXT Rage is expected to be a luxury electric motorcycle with a price in the $28,000-$30,000 range.

# Kitin Moto

Chinese-startup Kitin Moto is currently developing three models of electric motorcycles. The bikes will be offered in models with peak power levels of 11 kW (14.8 hp), 6 kW (8 hp) and 3 kW (4 hp). The bikes feature three innovative 1 kWh triangular shaped batteries and a chain drive mid-mount motor. The highest power bike is expected to be offered for pre-sale via crowdfunding in China later in 2019. This bike is expected to offer a range of 100 km (60 mi) at city speeds and a top speed of 120 km/h (75 mph). The lower power models are still in the design phase and are expected to follow the release of the 11 kW model.

# Fuell Flow

Fuell is a new electric two-wheeler startup founded in part by Erik Buell, a motorcycle pioneer who worked for Harley-Davidson before branching off and starting his own company Buell Motorcycles. That company was eventually purchased by Harley-Davidson before ultimately being discontinued. Now Buell is back with a new team and this time focusing on electric power. The company debuted two vehicles in early 2019: the Flow electric motorcycle and Fluid electric bicycle. The Flow will come in two power levels, 11 kW (14.8 hp) and 35 kW (47 hp). The motor will be mounted in the rear hub and supported by a single-sided swingarm. While Fuell's electric bicycle should be available by the end of 2019, don't expect the Flow to arrive before 2021.

# Evoke 6061

Evoke Motorcycles unveiled the design of their electric cruiser motorcycle in April of 2019. Known as the Evoke 6061, it uses a twin plate frame that is laser cut from sheets of T6-6061 aluminum. It should also feature Evoke's new Gen 2 batteries, which the company claims can be recharged from 0-85% in 15 minutes. The 6061 will also sport a 120 kW (160 hp) motor, which would make it one of the most powerful production motorcycles available, once it is released. Evoke estimates that they will begin production in late 2019. The project has already seen delays, so don't be surprised if this one isn't on the street until early 2020.

The goal of this section was to provide just a taste of yet to be released electric motorcycles and scooters. While 2019 is set to be a landmark year for the electric motorcycle industry, it is apparent that we are still in the early days of the rapidly expanding industry. As additional companies enter the market, and more riders discover the joy of electric motorcycles, new designs should begin pouring out over the next few years.

I, for one, have been amazed at the progress seen in the electric motorcycle industry over just the last several years. Despite a lack of recent major innovations in Li-ion battery technology, manufacturers have continued to develop increasingly popular electric two-wheelers. As battery technology continues to improve over the years, solid state batteries and other innovations will undoubtedly result in lighter, more powerful and more affordable electric motorcycles.

Soon as we enter the 2020's, you should expect to see even more impressive offerings from startups and established manufacturers alike.

And that should excite us all!

Fuell Flow

# Acknowledgments

As usual, my wife Sapir deserves the first acknowledgment. To her credit, she puts up with me and allows me to live a lifestyle where I can hop from electric bike to electric bike all day long. She also serves as my best sounding board for ideas and as my aesthetic advisor, making sure that the things I create look good after I've ensured that they work well. You should have seen the terrible cover I first designed for this book before she suggested its much better minimalist cover.

I also thank my parents, Ron and Kathy Toll, who raised me to follow my passions and never stop asking questions. Their emphasis on obtaining a broad and robust education while still learning the value of hard work and manual labor helped me become an engineer and tinkerer. While I'll always cherish my childhood memories of working on cool classic cars with my Dad, I also appreciate that he was every bit as jazzed when my interests led me towards electric vehicles. My parents also deserve credit for not worrying too terribly much while I zig-zagged through life in attempt to avoid taking a real job.

Speaking of avoiding a real job, sincere appreciation goes to Seth Weintraub for bringing me into the Electrek family. Reporting on the personal electric vehicle industry for Electrek has helped me learn even more about these amazing vehicles and travel the world in search of the most fascinating models in development and production. Thank you Seth for seeing the value in my two-wheeled EV work and giving me a larger platform to introduce these vehicles to the world.

In a roundabout way, I may also owe the majority of my writing career to my friend Elie Fuhrman. It was a particular conversation with him on one of our long Shabbat walks that, in part, helped set in motion a series of events that led me to where I am today.

Max Pless and Thorin Tobiassen were also there at the beginning of my electric bike career. Together in college we founded and ran an electric bicycle startup that served as the trailhead to this long and winding path I've traveled ever since. Thanks guys!

# About the Author

Micah Toll is a mechanical engineer and entrepreneur with over a decade of experience in the personal electric vehicle industry. Having ridden nearly every form of personal electric vehicle available, this book has been his passion project. Micah's other books, *The Ultimate DIY Ebike Guide, DIY Lithium Batteries* and *DIY Solar Power,* have sold tens of thousands of copies worldwide. In addition to his books, he has created countless hours of free educational online content covering electric bicycles, lithium-ion batteries and electric motorcycles. As a journalist for the electric vehicle news website Electrek, he has reported on many of the most important stories affecting the personal electric vehicle industry and helped to shape public perception of these important vehicles. Micah currently lives in Cambridge, MA with his beautiful wife Sapir and his dog Seven. And as you probably guessed, he's writing this bio in third person.

# Image credits

All images provided for use in this book belong to their respective copyright holders as listed below. My gratitude goes out to the following companies and individuals, listed in the order in which their images appear:

Zero – Images provided by Zero Motorcycles, www.ZeroMotorcycles.com
Harley-Davidson LiveWire – Image provided by Fred Lambert of Electrek, www.electrek.co
Evoke Urban Series – Images provided by Evoke Electric Motorcycles, www.EvokeMotorcycles.com
Lightning models – Images provided by Lightning Motorcycles, www.LightningMotorcycle.com
Energica models – Images provided by Energica Motor Company, www.EnergicaMotor.com
SuperSOCO TS, TC – Images provided by SuperSOCO, www.SuperSOCOmoto.com
SuperSOCO TC Max - Image provided by Fred Lambert of Electrek, www.electrek.co
Nuuk – Images provided by Nuuk, www.Nuuk-Europe.com
Fly Free Smart – Image provided by Fly Free, www.FlyFreeSmart.com
CSC City Slicker – Image provided by CSC Motorcycles of Azusa, California, www.CSCmotorcycles.com
Sol Motors – Image provided by Sol Motors, www.Sol-Motors.com
UBCO 2x2 – Image provided by UBCO, www.UBCObikes.com
Alta Redshift EXR – Image provided by Alta Motors (RIP)
CAKE Kalk OR – Image provided by CAKE, www.RideCAKE.com
Sur Ron MX – Image provided by Amped Motorcycles of Wales, UK, www.ampedmotorcycles.com
Kuberg Freerider – Image provided by Kuberg, www.Kuberg.com
KTM Freeride E-XC – Image provided by KTM, www.KTM.com
Electric Motion – Image provided by Electric Motion, www.Electric-Motion.fr
ONYX CTY and RCR – Image provided by ONYX, www.ONYXmotorbikes.com
Gogoro – Image provided by Gogoro, www.Gogoro.com
KYMCO Ionex – Images provided by KYMCO Ionex, www.IONEX.global
NIU – Images provided by NIU, www.NIU.com
SuperSOCO CUx – Image provided by SuperSOCO, www.SuperSOCOmoto.com
GenZe – image provided by GenZe, www.GenZe.com
Etergo AppScooter – Image provided by Etergo, www.etergo.com
BMW C Evolution – Image provided by BMW Motorrad, www.BMWmotorcycles.com
Vespa Elettrica – Image provided by Piaggio, www.PiaggioGroup.com
Flux EM1 – Image provided by Flux Mopeds, www.FluxMopeds.com
UJET – Images provided by UJET, www.UJET.com
Zapp i300 – Image provided by Zapp, www.ZappScooter.com
OjO – Image provided by OjO, www.OjOelectric.com
Doohan – Image provided by Doohan, www.Doohan-ev.com
Torrot – Image provided by Torrot, www.Torrot.com
Kumpan – Images provided by Kumpan Electric, www.Kumpan-electric.com
Govecs Schwalbe – Images provided by Govecs, www.GovecsGroup.com
Silence S01 – Image provided by Silence, www.Silence.eco
Unu – Image provided by Unu GmbH, www.UnuMotors.com
Vostok E7 – Image provided by Vostok, www.VostokElectric.com
Ather – Image provided by Ather Energy, www.AtherEnergy.com
Okinawa – Image provided by Okinawa Scooters, www.OkinawaScooters.com
RMK E2 – Image provided by RMK Vehicle Corporation, www.RMKvehicles.com
Tarform – Image provided by photographer/director Ryan Handt, www.RyanHandt.com
Curtiss – Image provided by Curtiss Motorcycles, www.CurtissMotorcycles.com
Ducati – Background image provided by Bart Heijt & Fernando Pastre, www.BartHeijtDesign.com
Novus – Image provided by Novus, www.NovusBike.com
Ural – Image provided by Ural Motorcycles, www.IMZ-Ural.com
Arc Vector – Image provided by Arc, www.ARCvehicle.com
Pursang – Image provided by Pursang Motorcycles, www.PursangMotorcycles.com
Honda – Images provided by Honda Motorcycles, www.Powersports.Honda.com
NXT Rage – Image provided by NXT Motors, www.NXTmotors.com
Kitin Moto – Image provided by Kitin Moto, www.KitinMoto.com
Fuell Flow – Image provided by Francois-Xavier Terny